Jesus

16 *Sermons to* Help You
KNOW HIM & LOVE HIM

REV. DR. HAROLD E. SALEM
OF *The Christian Worship Hour*

Dedicated to The First Baptist Church of Belle Fourche,
the First Baptist Church of Aberdeen,
and The Christian Worship Hour.
Thank you for allowing me to preach the beautiful name of Jesus.

CONTENTS

INTRODUCTION
My Mother

MY MOTHER, CLARA LOUISE SALEM, was born December 24, 1890. She taught school for eight years, and then was married to Mike Salem in June of 1920. She raised five children—four boys and one girl—and after they all left home, she renewed her teaching certificate and taught another eight years.

My earliest recollection was of Mother telling us about Jesus—about how kind he was, how he helped people, and how he died for our sins. She sang a lot while working. We had no electricity or running water, but she'd cook three meals a day for a family of five people plus one or two hired men. She'd wash all their clothes for them. How she got it all done, I have no idea. But I remember her singing the old hymns—such as "What a Friend We Have in Jesus," and "I Must Tell Jesus." Over and over again as a young boy I remember hearing her sing these words:

I must tell Jesus! I must tell Jesus!
I cannot bear my burden alone.

I've often thought, How could she have ever done it all? Yet in spite of the impossible work load, every night she would get us in bed, and then read a Bible story by lamplight, and say a prayer for us, and give us a kiss. And the story was always about Jesus.

She revered Jesus. She loved him, and she talked about him—about how Jesus loves us and helps us, and how he's our friend. I could see Jesus in my mother, in what she did and how she lived, and in how real Jesus was to her.

I remember one time she gave me a spanking. It was the only spanking I ever got. I was eight or nine years old. I used a slang word like "gosh" or "darn," which Mother said was the same as swearing or taking the Lord's name in vain. So she gave me a spanking, and it didn't amount to much, but I felt sorry for myself. So I went and sat down behind the cookstove and cried. In my tears, I finally got to praying to Jesus, and I said "Jesus, Jesus" over and over.

Well, my mother heard me, and it was too much for her. She rushed over, took me in her arms, and comforted me. Jesus answered my first prayer!

My love for my mother kept me out of a lot of trouble. Our hired men smoked and drank quite a bit, and I can see them yet, going out on the town Saturday night and coming home Sunday half drunk, with red eyes. But mother taught us that our body was a temple of the Holy Spirit, and over and over she told us not to smoke or drink or gamble. I never got into any of that, because I didn't want to let my mother down. I loved her so much. She believed in me, and I didn't want to let her down.

As she entered her nineties, her mind began to fail, and by her middle nineties, she had no memory. I was visiting with her once, just spending time with her, and I couldn't talk about the past because she didn't remember it. But at one point I asked my mother, "Do you remember Louise?" Louise was her only daughter. There were four of us boys, and Louise was the only girl. But no, she didn't remember Louise.

I asked, "Do you remember Stephen?" Stephen was the youngest and the baby of our family. But no, she didn't remember Stephen.

Then I asked, "Do you remember Harold?" I was the oldest, and I spent a lot of time in the house, helping my mother almost every day. I did the dishes with her, and I mopped the floors, and I made the beds. I was very close to her all my life. But she said, "No." She couldn't remember me at all.

I asked her one more question. "Mom, do you remember Jesus?"

She sat up straighter in her bed and raised her head. Her eyes brightened, and she said, "Oh yes, I remember Jesus."

All of this world had been taken away from her. All the treasures were gone. We never had much money, but it was gone. Her memories were gone, even of her children. But she still had Jesus.

I've preached more sermons on Jesus than on any other topic. I never get tired of preaching about Jesus, and I never get tired of thinking about Jesus. I never ever get tired of that old story, and who Jesus is, and how he helps us.

I've walked with Jesus for ninety years. And he's close, right next to me in my heart and my life. I don't hear his audible voice, and I've never seen a vision of him, but he speaks to me, and I know he's in my heart and my life. I'll have that feeling of certainty of his presence a lot of times when I need help in a situation that doesn't seem right, or I'm unsure exactly what I ought to be doing. I've known and walked with him for ninety years, and nothing can ever take that away.

It was through my mother that I fell in love with Jesus. That's why I'm so thrilled with this book. My love for Jesus came from my mother, and she is in this book.

PART I

The Person of Jesus

THE
WONDERFUL
NAME OF JESUS

Philippians 2:5-11

Let this mind be in you which was also in Christ Jesus, who, being in the form of God, did not consider it robbery to be equal with God, but made Himself of no reputation, taking the form of a bondservant, and coming in the likeness of men. And being found in appearance as a man, He humbled Himself and became obedient to the point of death, even the death of the cross. Therefore God also has highly exalted Him and given Him the name which is above every name, that at the name of Jesus every knee should bow, of those in heaven, and of those on earth, and of those under the earth, and that every tongue should confess that Jesus Christ is Lord, to the glory of God the Father.

THERE ARE NAMES THAT THRILL OUR SOULS, AND JUST to hear that name is music to our ears many times. To hear a certain person's name brings back many happy memories and joyful thoughts. Of course, all names don't do that, but some names do.

There's one name that always brings joy and peace and comfort. It always brings strength and happiness. That name is the subject of this chapter, and it's the wonderful and lovely name of Jesus.

Now, how would you describe that name? Where would you begin if you wanted to tell about that name? If you wanted to put into words what that name meant to you, how would you begin? It would be totally impossible. We just couldn't do it. We could just write volumes and still never plumb the depths of the wonderful, beautiful name of Jesus Christ.

That's what Paul talks about in this important passage where he said that God has highly exalted Jesus and given him a name which is above every name. Saint Paul says that at the name of Jesus, every knee is going to bow in heaven and earth and under the earth, and that every tongue is going to confess that Jesus Christ is Lord, to the glory of God the Father.

That's the way Paul talked about it. God has exalted Jesus, and so there is no name or no person that comes near to it. Furthermore, the day is going to come when all the world is going to fall down and worship Jesus Christ. They're going to fall prostrate before him and confess that he is indeed the Son of God, and that he is God.

People take his name in vain today. I hear so many times people cursing and taking in vain the name of Jesus. That's the devil's trick. Why don't they take some other name, like George Washington or Muhammad or somebody? But no, it's Jesus. That's the devil's attack against the Son of God. He's got the whole world talking about it. They make jokes about Jesus. They use his name flippantly and lightly.

But from heaven God declares that there is no name like Jesus Christ. If we're wise, we'll reverence that name, and we'll give it the place it deserves.

In the book of Ephesians, we have another picture of Jesus and of what God thinks about Jesus. In the first chapter of Ephesians we read of that same mighty power that raised Christ from the dead and seated him in the place of honor at God's right hand in heaven, far above any other king or ruler or dictator or leader (Ephesians 1:19-21). Yes, honor belonging to Jesus is far more glorious than that of anyone else, either in this world or in the world to come.

Then Paul goes on to say, "and God has put all things under his feet and made him supreme head of the church, which is his body filled with himself, the fullness of him who fills all in all" (Ephesians 1:22-23).

Here we're told that in Jesus Christ, God displayed his mightiest power—when after three days, he brought that body from the dead and he raised him up and let him walk around for forty days. Then he took him up into heaven, and Jesus Christ is seated at the right hand of God Almighty.

That's Jesus Christ, the one whom we worship, and the reason you're reading this. He is worthy of all our praise, and the Bible tells us that God placed Jesus at his own right hand and placed him over all the principalities and powers and all might and all dominion—and that includes Satan. Jesus Christ is far greater and more powerful than any earthly ruler or any spiritual ruler of the spirit world, including Satan.

If you want to see the power of God, look at the Soviet Union when it was one of the superpowers and people debated whether the United States or Russia was the greatest superpower. It looked like the Soviet Union would stand forever, or at least for many hundreds of years, like the Roman Empire did. But overnight, the Soviet Union dissolved and broke all to pieces. That's a nation that we were afraid of and spent billions of dollars to defend ourselves against, and it became like a helpless giant sprawling on the floor.

You see how great God is. He sets nations up, and when he says, "I'm done with you," or "You've gone far enough, and you've passed the mark," he puts them down. He has total control over nations and powers. That's our God.

All through the New Testament, God is exalting and uplifting his Son. God is always pleased with his Son. God is always calling attention to his Son. At the baptism of Jesus, God called out of heaven, "This is my beloved Son, in whom I am well pleased" (Matthew 3:17).

God broke the silence again at the Mount of Transfiguration, when he said, "This is my beloved Son in whom I am well pleased. Listen to him" (Luke 9:35). God has taken that name of Jesus, and he has exalted and uplifted it.

Consequently, it is a great conquering name. In the name of Jesus, we're going to be victorious. We see that all the time when people come out of sin and they receive Christ and they are made new creatures, new creations. Every time that happens, it's a miracle. It takes a great miracle to transform a human soul. You may have been transformed, just like I've been transformed, by the mighty power of Jesus Christ. That power then becomes alive within us.

It's a conquering name, and it is destined to rule over all of creation, however much that is. We don't even know for sure how much God created. We don't have any idea the size of the universe that God created when he just spoke it into existence. He just spoke the word, and it was there, and we don't even know where the ends of it are. It's countless light years away, and we don't even comprehend the length and the breadth of the universe.

The name Jesus was given to him first of all by the angel Gabriel, when he announced to Mary, "Thou shalt conceive and bring forth a Son, and thou shall call his name Jesus" (Matthew 1:20-21). When Joseph was trying to decide whether or not he was actually going to take Mary to be his wife after he was betrothed to her, an angel came to him and said, "You take Mary to be your wife, and that Son who is going to be born of her, conceived by the Holy Spirit of God—you must name him Jesus."

That blessed name of Jesus was carried by our Lord throughout his earthly life, and it was often used for him by the apostles after his ascension. We use it today and we sing about it today—the wonderful, wonderful name of Jesus. It's referred to again and again in the New Testament epistles and especially in the book of Hebrews. It stands for the very highest type of being—Jesus Christ, who is over the whole realm of existence. This is the name that is above every name.

There's going to come a day when every knee in heaven is going to bow to Jesus. Well, that's not hard, because heaven is filled with people who are there because they love Jesus and they've already bowed to him. But all the people on earth are also going to have to bow to him. And those people who refuse to believe that Jesus Christ is anything, and those who take his name in vain, and those who have refused him again and again, are going to kneel down and admit that he is the Son of God.

Now, that's not going to save them. They're just going to have to do it, because God Almighty is making them kneel down. But the way the knee goes, that doesn't matter. It's how does the heart go. Those people will be so filled with rage and hatred that they have to bow down to somebody they've despised. No, bowing down will never save their soul, and they'll go on to perdition.

The Bible says that even in Hades they're going to bow down before the name of Jesus. Can you imagine Adolf Hitler and Joe Stalin and old Mussolini kneeling down at the name of Jesus in Hades? Every criminal, every evil person, along with every morally good person that hasn't received Jesus Christ—they're all going to be there with Hitler and Mussolini and all the rest of those creeps, and they're going to have to kneel down. At last, the record is going to be set straight, and they're going to see that Jesus Christ is the King of kings and the Lord of lords. Heaven and earth and hell are going to admit that, and God's going to see to it.

There you have it. The whole realm of existence is going to bow down and confess that Jesus Christ is almighty God. So what do we do?

First of all, let's take some lessons from this name. Let's take instruction, and let's see how we ought to live and how we ought to behave. It's the highest name, the very highest name, in all the world. That wonderful name of Jesus shows us how our attitude toward life ought to be.

That name teaches us that we need to be gentle and kind and loving, and we need to be meek and lowly, and we need to be forgiving. That's how Jesus lived.

Now, the world teaches the opposite. I remember a time over fifty years ago when a man came up to me after a service, and he says, "I'm going to tell you two things I'll never do." He says, "I'll never give ten percent to God, and I'll never forgive my enemies." I asked the pastor of that church some years later, "Did that man ever turn?" He says, "He never turned. He died that way." That's the way of the world.

In the world, we sum it up in the phrase "survival of the fittest." We see that out in creation, in the animal world, where the strong will take advantage of the weak, and the quick will take advantage of the slow, and where the smart will take advantage of those that aren't so smart. They move with great brute force and they trample mercilessly the weaker wherever they are. That which can conquer all is the one with the strength and the power and the might, and its called survival of the fittest.

The gentle and the kind and the meek and the lowly—they're the ones beaten down and trodden down. They're the ones who are oppressed and eradicated. It's there in the animal world, and it carries over into the human world, man and beast alike. You get what you can. You go through and you take everybody once and the easy ones twice. Talking around town, you hear that and see it. It's the man with the muscle, the sinew, the man with the giant's grip, the crushing blow, the Atlas type of man. He's the one to win the day—the man with power, brute force, big and mighty. The one that can take advantage of somebody, of the weaker. That's who the world says is going to succeed.

But there is some instruction to be taken from the name of Jesus. That instruction is that the gentle and the kind and the forgiving and the loving and the self-denying, and those who help others—they're the winners, and the others are the losers. It isn't brute strength that finally wins.

Or sometimes people think the winner will be the intellectual type, the scientist who rules through the intellectual power and acumen, the sharp, the clever one who puts man on the moon and he puts these vehicles on Mars and other planets, and he's so wise. They say that's the one to win the day.

Or some will say the man of wealth will win the day. They'll always ask, How much money does he have? They're not asking what kind of a man he is. They don't say, How kind is he? They don't say, What kind of a father is he? They don't ask how many people he has helped. They don't seek to know all the good that he did for Christ, and all the self-denial he practiced. No. How much money does he have? That's the thing the world goes after.

Jesus comes along and he tells the world something very startling. The Lord Jesus comes along, and he's sweet and gentle, and he's kind and meek. He serves others. He stoops down to wash the feet of others. He's forgiving, and he's lowly, and he's loving and kind. He's the winner. He's the one that's going to have the final word. You mark it down. He's the one they're going to kneel to and bow to: Jesus Christ the humble.

We need to take instruction from this wonderful life of Christ. It's good to worship in God's house. It's good to set aside a time to worship Christ and think about the things of God, and not so much about the things of the world. In the many years of my ministry, I've seen television come on the scene, and I'm going to tell you, television has been a terrible, terrible scourge in this world. I see things on that television that they're advertising or promoting, trying to whet your appetite. You cannot believe what they run before children's eyes. Television has done a terrible thing to America, along with pornography and all the rest. And I want to tell you, television has hurt the church of Jesus Christ, because that garbage filters in. In spite of what we think and want, it gets into us. We need to get away from that and get back to Jesus Christ, to think the way he thinks and love the way he loves and forgive the way he forgives and forgets sins. We pray, Forgive us our sins as we forgive those who sin against us. What in the world is happening? We want God to forgive us the way we forgive others, but we don't forgive others. What's going on here? We need to take a lesson from Jesus.

We also need to take encouragement from the name of Jesus. All of us at one time or another have wondered and thought in our heart what God was like. We've just wondered what was going on in our life, and we wonder if God hears us. We've had some difficult things happen, and we wonder why. What is the meaning of it all?

We need to realize that there's a God who loves us and who has a purpose and reason for everything we see in life. I think we have to reason also, as the Bible says, that there's inequity in the world. There's sin in the world, and there's evil. We're under a curse, and hard things happen to good people because that curse touches all humanity. But there is a God, and you can take encouragement in the fact that this God loves you, and you can trust him and lean upon him.

Finally, we ought to exult in the name of Jesus. We ought to learn that. We ought to learn first of all to pray in the name of Jesus. There's power in prayer, so pray in the name of Jesus. He says that if we believe in him and trust in him, he will hear us and answer our prayer. Pray in the name of Jesus. Follow that name. Live that name when you go out to work or to school, and wherever you go. Live the name of Jesus.

Let others see Jesus in you. Speak of that name. Talk about Jesus. If you're a Sunday school teacher, don't ever let a lesson go by without talking about Jesus. If you're a preacher, don't ever preach a sermon without talking about Jesus. If you're a parent, talk about Jesus in front of your children just as though he was a friend right there. As you witness as a Christian, talk about Jesus. Jesus isn't somebody you meet on Sunday but don't talk about till the next week.

Talk about Jesus, and see Jesus in the sunrise or the sunset, or in the flowers or whatever is before you. See the Lord Jesus. Speak of that name.

Then finally, worship that name. Lean on that name. Trust that name. Reverence that name. Adore that name. Never speak lightly of it. Just speak of that name that is so precious and so wonderful.

G. Campbell Morgan has written a passage I've just got to share with you. It's just too good, better than anything I could ever write. G. Campbell Morgan was an Anglican minister in England for many years. He was a brilliant man who preached in America at times, but mostly in England. And he wrote this:

> The name of Jesus was given before. When he was to come into the world, an angel messenger said, "Thou shall call his name JE-SUS. For it is he that shall save his people from their sins." It was then a prophetic name. The mother was to utter it as expressing the hope of her own heart and all the human race, which she represented. *Thou shall call his name Jesus.* It marked a purpose. It uttered

a prophecy. It sang of a hope as Mary, with a babe on her bosom, bending over him in sweet maternal love, in obedience to the angel command first called him Yeshua, Jesus.

He went his way. He lived his life and he went his way and died his death. He went his way and broke the bars of death asunder. He went his way shining back to the everlasting spaces. Then he was invested forevermore with the same sweet name that his mother had uttered in obedience to the angelic message as a prophecy. Now the prophecy of the name is fulfilled. Let heaven recognize it. Let earth know it. Let hell tremble at it. Yeshua, Jesus, human Savior, the divine Lord of life forever and forevermore. God gave him the same sweet name to make the infinite music of all the coming ages when he exalted him on his right hand.

Jesus, the name above every name, above every other name in preciousness. No name is so dear to the ear of God as the name of the one who did his will, accomplished his purpose, and wrought out his infinite plan of salvation. No name is so dear to man as that. There are other names very dear to us, the names that become dear, according to the persons for whom they stand. I could name human names that some of you find no music in, that thrill with music for me. But bring me the sweetest name of them all and the dearest and utter it. Then say this one word, Jesus, and all the earthly music becomes dim and dies away. The earthly glow was cold.

> Jesus, thou joy of loving hearts,
>   thou fount of light, thou light of men,
>   from the best bliss that earth imparts
>   we turn unfilled to thee again.

Oh, men and women, there is no name in all the world so sweet as this to the world. Away on the lonely sea tonight, some soul will sing it, and it will be a haven of refuge.

In the midst of the awful loneliness of the crowded city, some tired hark will utter it, and it will be a pillow of rest. Out yonder, on the veldt in Africa, some young man tempted and tried, will hear it and will win. There is no name like it. You know it, you do not want me to argue it. It is above every name because it is the name that stands for the manifestation of such love as men have never dreamed of. His love is stronger than death or hell. Love that reaches to the lowest, love that lifts to the highest. Love that lasts forever. Shakespeare sang of earthly loves, and said,

> Love is not love
> that alters when it alteration finds.

Did you ever find any earthly love that quite rose to that level? If you want to find a love that alters not when it alteration finds, I bring you back to Jesus. He loved me—I cannot tell you why, but he loved me. And in my heart of hearts, I know it. And in spite of all that I have been, he loves me still. There's no one else like this in love, the name above every name.[1]

What have you done with that name? Have you taken that name into your heart and your life, and do you love it, and do you obey it, and do you revel in it? The wonderful, wonderful name of Jesus.

Dear heavenly Father, we just don't seem to be worthy even to mention that name. We just thank you for Jesus. Thank you that he went to that old rugged cross, paid for our sins, and loves us in spite of our sins. When we come to you, you take them all away. You never hold a grudge. You never hold it over our head, but by your grace, you forgive us of all our sins and all our shortcomings. After we're saved, we sin on, and yet you forgive us and you forget. Thank you for Jesus! Amen.

CHRIST CAME TO REVEAL THE INVISIBLE GOD

John 1:1-18

In the beginning was the Word, and the Word was with God, and the Word was God. He was in the beginning with God. All things were made through Him, and without Him nothing was made that was made. In Him was life, and the life was the light of men. And the light shines in the darkness, and the darkness did not comprehend it.

There was a man sent from God, whose name was John. This man came for a witness, to bear witness of the Light, that all through him might believe. He was not that Light, but was sent to bear witness of that Light. That was the true Light which gives light to every man coming into the world.

He was in the world, and the world was made through Him, and the world did not know Him. He came to His own, and His own did not receive Him. But as many as received Him, to them He gave the right to become children of God, to those who believe in His name: who were born, not of blood, nor of the will of the flesh, nor of the will of man, but of God.

And the Word became flesh and dwelt among us, and we beheld His glory, the glory as of the only begotten of the Father, full of grace and truth.

John bore witness of Him and cried out, saying, "This was He of whom I said, 'He who comes after me is preferred before me, for He was before me.'"

And of His fullness we have all received, and grace for grace. For the law was given through Moses, but grace and truth came through Jesus Christ. No one has seen God at any time. The only begotten Son, who is in the bosom of the Father, He has declared Him.

THESE VERSES IN JOHN 1 DEAL WITH THE PURPOSE OF the incarnation, the object of the incarnation. And when we talk about the coming of the incarnation, we simply mean the coming of Christ, the Son of God, who is God himself, and how he came into the world and he took upon himself the form of a man.

He took upon him human flesh, without sin. And that's what incarnation means; it means enfleshment. So when God took on a body of flesh for us, in the form of his Son, Jesus Christ was in the flesh, but he was sinless. He's the only sinless person that ever lived and walked on this earth. And so this wonderful Lord Jesus came.

This scripture talks about this wonderful Savior, and it tells us, "No man has seen God at any time. The only begotten Son, which is in the bosom of the Father, he hath declared him." You could translate this verse to read, "No man has seen God at any time. The only begotten Son, subsisting in the bosom of the Father, he hath told him how." That is, he has let us know God in all of his fullness, because Jesus is God.

So we have the holy Trinity: God the Father, God the Son, God the Holy Spirit. They all are God, and Jesus Christ is not only the Son of God; he *is* God. Who is it that created the earth and all there is, and who holds all things together? As Paul says of Jesus Christ, "He is before all things, and by him all things consist" (Colossians 1:17)—that is, in him

27

all things hold together, and they don't all fly apart—all the planets and stars, and everything else.

God did that through the power of the Lord Jesus Christ. Sometimes we hear people say, "Well, I'd like to know what God is like." They say that nobody's seen God at any time, and they'd just like to know what he's like. They say, I wonder what he wants me to do, and I wish I could understand him better; I wish I knew what the mind of God was; I wish I knew his view on certain things.

Well, let me tell you something, dear friend. If you want to know God, you just get to know Jesus Christ, because the Lord Jesus Christ has perfectly manifested God to the world. If you know the Lord Jesus, then you know God, because God is precisely and exactly like Jesus Christ, the wonderful Savior.

There is but one God in all the universe. There are false gods all over the place. Everybody's got some kind of a god, all over the world, for all times. But there's only one true God, and he's the God who's revealed to us in Jesus Christ.

So if you want to know the holiness of God, then take a look at the holiness of Jesus. If you want to know the righteousness of God, then take a look at the righteousness of Jesus Christ. If you want to look at the purity of God, then examine the purity in the life of the Lord Jesus. If you want to know the compassion of God, then look at the life of the Lord and the compassion that he showed all the time. He saw the people scattered about as sheep not having a shepherd, and his heart went out to them.

He's a wonderful Savior, this Jesus. Now that's God. That's the same as God, he has the same compassion. If you want to see the love of God, then see the love of God shed abroad in the life and the walk of Jesus Christ.

And let me add one other thing. If you want to see the hatred of God, then you see the hatred of Jesus Christ. Immediately you might say, Well, when did Jesus ever hate? When did God ever hate?

Well, he hates sin, for one thing, doesn't he? Jeremiah says, in 44:4, "God cries out, 'Oh, do not do this abominable thing that I hate!'" So God hates. He hates sin. He hates hypocrisy. He hates uncleanness. He hates impurity. He hates everything sinful. So Jesus Christ has a perfect hatred toward these things.

You may think that God loves everybody and everything; he does love us, and he wants us to turn to him, but he hates sin. And you say, Well how can it be that God loves me and hates me at the same time? Well did you ever have children? That's exactly what it is. God is hurt when we sin, because he hates sin, and he hates to see it in our lives. Preachers these days have forgotten about the great God of judgment who hates sin, and who declares that no sinful thing will ever enter heaven. Do you ever think about the anger of God? Well, we never think he'll be angry at us, but in Psalm 7:11 we're told that God is angry with the wicked every day.

So the next question is, Who are the wicked? Well, the wicked are the wicked. They're those who are outside of Christ, those who have rejected Jesus Christ. God hates them because he gave his Son, he gave everything he had, he gave everything heaven had, and he gave Jesus as a gift, and you throw the gift in the garbage. You stomp on it, and you reject the Lord Jesus Christ. But you're dealing with the Son of God. You're rejecting his Son. He did everything he can, and you're rebuffing

God. You're saying you don't care, and you'll laugh in his face. You take his name in vain, and you live like the dogs and the hogs. They don't even live that way. So yes, God hates sin. But he loves us also, and he's angry with those in sin, and we have to come to him.

I'm going to tell you something. The wonderful love of God is there, and he loves you in all of your sin. He loves you and wants you to come to him, but there's going to be a day when that love ends. And that love is going to end the day you die.

Because after death, there's the judgment, and if you die with God's displeasure and hatred, you can never get to heaven. And you say, Well, God would never keep me out of heaven. But he isn't keeping you out of heaven; you're keeping yourself out. It's your choice. That's why we preach over and over and over, and we want you to come to Jesus. You say, No, no. You're choosing hell, that's all you're doing. So say yes.

I know that every time we preach, there are people who come to Jesus all over the world. And I know there's three things that happen when we preach the Word of God. Three things. There are those who will reject him outright, and say, We'll have nothing to do with him. And then there are those who say, We'll consider it at another time. They put it off. Then there's a third class, and they open their heart to Jesus.

How do you open your heart to Jesus? Jesus tells us in Revelation 3:20, "Behold, I stand at the door and knock." That's the door of your heart—not your head, but your heart.

Right now, I'm just sure that somewhere, someone is reading this, and right now you're feeling, "I want Jesus. I don't want the wrath of God, I want the love of God. I want Jesus." And he says to you, "I stand at the door and knock. If any person opens the door, I will come in, and

I'll fellowship with him." But he tells us that he will never come in unless you open the door.

So if you go into a Christless eternity, it's your choice, not God's. Peter tells us that God is not willing that any should perish, but that all should come to repentance (2 Peter 3:9). And so that's God.

But now listen again to this scripture from John 1. It tells us no man has seen God at any time. "The only begotten Son, which is in the bosom of the Father, he hath declared him."

Paul was writing to young Timothy, and this is what he said: "And without controversy, great is the mystery of godliness. God was manifest in the Spirit, seen of angels, preached among the nations, believed on in the world, and received up into glory" (2 Timothy 3:16). And in Hebrews 1:3, we read this about Jesus Christ— "who, being the brightness of his glory, and the express image of his person [that is, of the person of God], and upholding all things by the word of his power, when he had by himself purged our sins, sat down at the right hand of the Majesty on high."

These passages are telling us about Jesus. He came down to this world, born of a virgin, and he grew to manhood, as a man in the flesh. His flesh was sinless, but then all of a sudden it became wicked flesh, because he took *our* sins in his own body and soul. He took the sins of the world in the garden at Gethsemane, on the way to the cross. That's why he shed great drops of blood, because he was taking our sin into that holy, sinless, spotless body and soul of Jesus Christ. He was taking the sins of all the world for all time.

We cannot imagine it. It was such a horrible, terrible thing. Then he was nailed to the cross, and his Father in heaven turned his back on his own Son, because he would not countenance sin. Even the Son had to hide his face, it was such a terrible thing. And he did it for you, and he did it for me.

Yet people say, "Oh, I don't care," and they take his name in vain, and they slough him off. But God tells us to come to Jesus, because Jesus is the picture of God.

Jesus said in John 10:30, "I and my Father are one." They're the same. It's the holy Trinity. Then in John 14:9, when his disciples were asking Jesus how to find God, he said, "Have I been so long time with you, and yet hast thou not known me, Philip? He that has seen me, has seen the Father." That's what Jesus is saying. "He that has seen me has seen the Father."

Oh, friend, how we ought to honor the Lord Jesus Christ! We ought to exalt and revere his precious name. We ought to uphold his life in our life in every way we can. We ought to worship him and think of him constantly. We want to give ourselves to him fully and completely. We ought to say, "I don't want anything between me and my Lord Jesus Christ. I want him to rule in my life, I want him to have complete control of my life, so I have no will of my own but the will of the Lord Jesus Christ." That's what we ought to pray.

I just tremble at some people who say, "Oh, that's all right, God is so good that he'll let you in. He's so loving and so kind, he can never ever turn you away."

I heard one man discussing the electric chair, and he said, "You can't think of Jesus turning on the electric current, can you?" Well I'm going to tell you, when you reject Jesus Christ, you're going to have to face the Christless eternity. That's how it's going to end.

I don't understand how Jesus could make it any plainer than he does in John 5:23. He says, "He that honoreth not the Son honoreth not the Father which sent him." You're sinning against God, and you're sinning all the way into a Christless eternity.

But when you read the Bible, we find people who did see God. Take for instance Adam and Eve. They walked in the garden of Eden, and they were sinless; they had no sin until they committed the sin of eating the fruit, of disobeying God. That's what it was. It wasn't drunkenness, or anything else, it was disobedience to God. They walked with him, and they talked with him, but they never saw God in the fullness of his spirit. God is a spirit, and those that worship him must worship him in spirit and in truth. God is a spirit, and he's real. We can't see God, but we will someday. We'll never see him on this side, in the flesh.

Or take Abraham and his vision: "The Lord appeared unto Abraham at the oaks of Mamre. And he sat at his tent door in the heat of the day, and then Abraham lifted up his eyes and behold, three men stood by him, and when he saw them, he ran to meet them. And he said, 'My Lord, if I now have found favor in thy sight, pass me not away, I pray thee, for thy servant.'" That's in the opening verses of Genesis 18. Then see what happens in 18:33, after they've been having fellowship together: "And the Lord went his way as soon as he had talked with Abraham, and Abraham returned unto his place." It was an encounter that Abraham had with God. But that's before the incarnation, before the enfleshment, when God comes in the form of a man.

Moses had an encounter with God; you know the story, when Moses speaks to God in Exodus 33, and he's talking to God on the mount. He says, "I beseech thee, show me thy glory," and God says, "I will make all my goodness pass before thee. I will proclaim the name of the Lord before thee. I will be gracious with whom I will be gracious. I will show mercy on whom I will show mercy." And he said, "Thou canst not see my face. For there shall no man see me and live." And the Lord said, "Behold, there is a place by me. Thou shalt stand upon a rock, and it shall be, and it shall come to pass, while my glory passeth by, that I will put thee in a cleft of the rock. I will cover thee with my hand while I pass by, and I will take away my hand, and thou shalt see my back. And my face, thou shalt not see." Moses never did see God. He just saw a glimpse of the back of God, this wonderful God.

Ezekiel had visions of all sorts, and yet he never saw God face to face. In seminary, they call these appearances in the Bible theophanies. It means that in the Old Testament, God came to people in different forms. For instance, to Abraham, God came as a man. To Daniel, God came to him as an angel. To Ezekiel, God came to him in marvelous appearance. To the three Hebrew children in the fiery furnace, he came as just a man walking with them. But always remember this: God is a spirit, and they that worship him, worship a spirit in truth. A spirit cannot be seen with the regular eyes. We cannot see a spirit with our mortal eyes, and so you have never seen a spirit, and you'll never see God until we meet God face to face on the other side.

When Jesus was here, people did not see the deity, but they did see God in the form of flesh, in the flesh of the Lord Jesus. We're told in 2 Corinthians 5:19 that God was in Christ, reconciling the world unto himself. So here's God Almighty. When you talk about Jesus, you talk about him as the Son of God, but you talk about him also as God. He is God.

John tells us, in John 1:18, "No man has seen God at any time. The only begotten Son, which is in the bosom of the Father, he has declared him." That is, Jesus has come among us and declared him. Now we know what God is like, exactly what God is like. We know because of Jesus's perfect image of him. God tabernacled among us in Christ, he tented among us, so we could know this wonderful God. Sometimes people say, "If you see Jesus, you've seen God." No, you've seen a revelation of God. You've never seen God in his full deity.

Jesus reveals God in the flesh, and we see the flesh but we don't see God. No man has seen God at any time. When this same John has a wonderful vision, he gets to talk with Jesus, and talk about him. It's been maybe sixty years since Jesus ascended into heaven, and now John is an old man. He writes in 1 John 4:12, "No man hath seen God at any time."

John writes this after all of his experiences, and being close to Jesus Christ, and walking with Christ. Wasn't it to John that Jesus said, "Take care of my mother?" Wasn't it John who leaned his head on his breast with that great love? Well, John is an old man now, and after being that close to Jesus and all of his experiences, he says, "But I've never seen God. I've never seen the deity, and I never will until I pass over there."

This teaches us, then, that no man can ever see deity. When men saw Jesus, they saw a man like unto themselves, except without sin. But he really was not like them, for he was the holy one of God. He was separate, because God was dwelling in him, but you never see that great deity of Jesus Christ.

Why did Jesus come to earth? He came to show us the way, to be an example for us. He shows us how we can live for him, and walk with him, and get to know God personally. But we'll never see God in all of his deity and all of his glory.

We have so many friends who have passed away, and the older you get the more you have, and these departed believers are seeing God now. They have spiritual eyes. Those mortal eyes are now immortal eyes, and they see Jesus, and they see God in all of his glory.

Someday, we have that coming. But the beautiful thing about it is, when we walk with Jesus, we're walking with God and when we walk with Jesus, we have all that we need. We don't need anything else, because he satisfies all of our needs. Our wonderful, dear Savior. The world is searching. And Isaiah says, "The wicked are like the troubled sea, whose waters continually cast up mire and dirt. There is no peace, my God sayeth, to the wicked." (Isaiah 57:20). When he talks about the wicked, he means the unbeliever, the one who has rejected Jesus Christ. There is no peace, that's why there's craziness in the world. So many are running here and there, to and fro, crazy like. They don't have real contentment, because they don't have the Savior.

If we're walking with the Lord Jesus in fellowship and deep love, then we'll find that God is going to lay upon our hearts that we want others to know Jesus. We'll have that desire to make him known, or we'll help to make him known, and we'll pray. We can't all preach, and we can't all sing, but we can all pray, and we can all give something, and we can all tell our friends. We're reaching out to bring those people to Christ, the wonderful Lord Jesus Christ. When we walk with him, we'll find that all our needs are supplied, all our needs.

We're told that in Christ "dwelleth all the Godhead bodily." When you have Jesus, you have God. When you have God, you have all that you need. God takes care of everything.

An unknown poet wrote about it in these words:

In the heart of London city, amid the dwellings of the poor,
these bright golden words were uttered: I have Christ, what want
    I more?
Spoken by a lonely woman, dying on a garret floor,
having not one earthly comfort: I have Christ, what want I more?
He who heard them ran to fetch her something from the world's
    great store.
It was needless; died she saying, I have Christ, what want I more?
But her words will live forever, I repeat them o'er and o'er,
God delights to hear me saying, I have Christ, what want I more?
Look away from earth's attractions, friend, those joys will soon be
    o'er;
rest not until thy heart exclaimeth, I have Christ, what want I
    more?

Do you have Christ? Do you have Jesus? You don't have Jesus in your heart until you ask him in. John's Gospel tells us this about Jesus: "As many as received him, to them gave he power to become the children of God." (John 1:12). You have to receive him. Have you received him? He's standing right at your heart's door right now, and you could just say yes.

You may say, "I don't know how to receive Jesus, I can't see him, I can't talk to him, I can't handle him, he's not here. How can I receive something I can't see?" Well, all you need to do is just know that he's there. It's as if he knocks on the door of your house, and you say, "Come in." That's how you receive him. You open the door, you say, "Come in." So you open your heart's door, you say, "Jesus, come in." And Jesus says, "If any man asks me, I'll open the door, I will come in." And then when he comes in, that's receiving Jesus.

And then you tell him, "Dear Jesus, I've sinned against you." And he knows that. He knows every thought we have that has been sinful. Talk with him about your sins. He wants us to confess, and say, "I've sinned against you, dear Lord Jesus. I've sinned against you, God, and I ask you to come into my heart and take away my sins." And the blood of Jesus Christ cleanses us from all sin.

Then you tell him, "I'll make you the Lord of my life. If you're good enough to save my soul, you're good enough to lead me, and I'll follow you all the days of my life. I'll turn from anything that I know to be wrong, and I'll start doing the thing that you're laying on my heart. I'll follow you the best I can." You'll never be perfect, but you stumble along and he'll always be with you.

Dear heavenly Father, we just want to thank you for the multitudes of people that right now, are praying that prayer, and asking you into their heart. And how heaven must rejoice when the many precious souls come to you. We believe that's happening, right now. Lord, we want to pray for the children today, the little children. And the young people, oh God how terrible the temptations they have. And those in prison, Lord, we think of them, and just pray that you'll help them to be a witness for you, to take you into their lives. You love them, you died for them just as much as you did for anybody. You want them to come to you, and help them to open their heart to Jesus. And then the shut-ins, and the people that can't get out, and on beds of sickness. Help them to know that you're there, and that you'd never leave them or forsake them. And we'll give you the praise and thanks, in Jesus's name. Amen.

JESUS, THE SAME YESTERDAY, TODAY, AND FOREVER

Hebrews 13:5-14

Let your conduct be without covetousness; be content with such things as you have. For He Himself has said, "I will never leave you nor forsake you." So we may boldly say: "The Lord is my helper; I will not fear. What can man do to me?"

Remember those who rule over you, who have spoken the word of God to you, whose faith follow, considering the outcome of their conduct. Jesus Christ is the same yesterday, today, and forever. Do not be carried about with various and strange doctrines. For it is good that the heart be established by grace, not with foods which have not profited those who have been occupied with them.

We have an altar from which those who serve the tabernacle have no right to eat. For the bodies of those animals, whose blood is brought into the sanctuary by the high priest for sin, are burned outside the camp. Therefore Jesus also, that He might sanctify the people with His own blood, suffered outside the gate. Therefore let us go forth to Him, outside the camp, bearing His reproach. For here we have no continuing city, but we seek the one to come.

LLOYD DOUGLAS WAS THE AUTHOR OF A VERY POPULAR novel titled *The Robe,* which you may have heard of or read. He also wrote other novels. The story is told that when Lloyd Douglas attended college, he lived in a boarding house, and in that same boarding house there lived a retired professor of music who lived on the first floor and was confined to a wheelchair.

Douglas said that each morning he would stick his head into the old professor's room and say, "Well, what's the good word?" Without fail, the old professor would pick up his tuning fork, tap it on the side of the wheelchair, and say, "That's middle C. It was middle C yesterday. It will be middle C tomorrow. It will be middle C a thousand years from now." And he would add, "The tenant upstairs sings flat. The piano across the hall is out of tune. But my friend, that is middle C."

That's what the writer of the book of Hebrews was saying when he said, "Jesus Christ is the same yesterday, today, and forever." Jesus Christ is the middle C of eternity. He always was, he always is, and he always will be this great Jesus Christ.

Now that's hard to imagine, because we live in a world of change. As the old hymn "Abide with Me" says, "Change and decay in all around I see." We see it. Health changes. Customs change. Styles change. Women are going crazy to keep up with the styles. Even neckties change. They had to be real broad, then they had to be real narrow. They keep changing them. Attitudes change. Weather changes. Relationships change. Seasons change. We change.

The whole world was changed September 11, 2001. The world was forever changed. It was changed by less than two dozen men. And they changed the world. The perspectives of life were changed, and daily living was effected. The global economy recoiled from the effects of the terrorist attack that day. A new term came into being, a term I didn't even know: Ground Zero. I didn't know what Ground Zero was, but I know it now, and everybody knows it, because of those few men who changed all of the world.

So we wonder where we can turn. We wonder where we can go, in a world that's in such flux, until we hear God out of heaven say, "Jesus Christ. He is the same yesterday, today, and forever." Friend of mine, that's what we need.

Like the old music professor, we need a middle C. We need a constant. We need something that's always there and never changes or moves, and that's exactly what we have in Jesus Christ. He is the same Jesus Christ I learned about nearly ninety years ago at my mother's knee. He's the same one who has always been. He's never changing. He's forever the same. He is the eternal Son of God.

It's like a river flowing at the foot of a mountain. The river flows and is changing all the time, hour by hour and day by day and year by year and age by age. That river is always and forever changing, but that mountain never changes a bit. It's the same today as it was yesterday, and as it will be in the days to come. That's a picture of humanity, my friend.

Humanity is like that river that's always changing, always different. But Jesus Christ is like that mountain. He never changes. He's always the same. You can depend upon him yesterday, today, and forever. So in the old Isaac Watts hymn "O God, Our Help in Ages Past," there's the line that goes, "Time, like an ever-rolling stream, bears all its sons away." But not so Jesus Christ

This wonderful scripture is taken from the book of Hebrews, and the major theme of that whole book is the unchanging Christ, the immutable Christ, the forever Christ—the one who never changes but is always the same. It's all summed up in these words: He is the same yesterday, today, and forever.

The writer of the book of Hebrews makes a contrast to show this, to point this out. He points out first of all that we have a changeless Christ, but also a changing universe. So he writes (in Hebrews 1:11-12), "They shall perish but thou remainest, and they shall all wax old as doth a garment, and as a vesture shalt thou fold them up, and they shall be changed. But thou art the same, and thy years fail not." Nature changes, but Christ doesn't change.

The writer goes on and talks about our Redeemer. Christ is our High Priest. He talks about the priests in the Old Testament. The priests were always dying, and they had to get another priest. The high priest would be there a little while, then he would die, and again they need another priest. Then came Jesus Christ, and once and for all we have no more succession of priests. It ended when Christ came, because he never changes, and he'll never die, and never end.

The writer of Hebrews also makes a contrast between the kingdoms of this world and the kingdom of God. He looks at the kingdoms of this world, and they come and they go. How many countless kingdoms has this world had?

Look at the Roman Empire. It stood for a thousand years, and it took years and years before that thing collapsed and finally disintegrated, but it did. Or consider the Soviet Union. It was next to the United States in power, and some thought maybe it was actually more powerful than the United States. And it is gone, *gone*—and it didn't take a hundred years. It went so fast that we hardly realize it isn't there anymore. But it's gone.

The nations come and the nations go. But listen to this great God Almighty in his kingdom. Isaiah talked about it, and he says, "Of the increase of his government and peace, there shall be no end, upon the throne of David and upon his kingdom, to order it and establish it with judgment and with justice from henceforth even forever. The zeal of the Lord of Hosts will perform this" (Isaiah 9:7). Earthly kingdoms come and go, but the kingdom of God is here and will never end.

So let's look at Jesus today and look at him in a threefold way, three ways in which he never changes. He never changes in his person. He never changes in his personality, his teachings. He never changes in his redemption.

Look at him as a person. Somebody once wrote, "All that he is today, he was yesterday. All that he was yesterday, he is today. All that he will be tomorrow, he is today. And all that he is today, he will be forever." The same yesterday, today, and forever.

Look at yesterday. How far does that go back? What does yesterday embrace? Where does yesterday start? Where did it come from? Well, the Scripture says that before the mountains were brought forth he had formed the earth and the world, Christ was the same then. Before there even was an earth, before there was any creation, Jesus Christ is back there yesterday, way back there. Before there was time or people or anything, he is there.

Yesterday began when the morning stars sang together and all the sons of God shouted for joy. He was the same when Abraham of old rejoiced to see his day, and Moses came from Mount Sinai. Jesus is just the same, exactly the same. He's the same as when your mothers and fathers taught you in Sunday school about Jesus. He's always the same. How do I know that? Because the Scriptures tell us he is the same yesterday, today, and forever.

Today, Jesus Christ is with us. Jesus Christ is unchangeable as a teacher of divine truth. We hear this, and we sometimes wonder, "What can I really know?" We have so many books, so many teachings. We have the Quran, and we have everything else. Who's right? Who's wrong? Who do you go by? Can we really know anything?

"What is truth?" Pilate said. What ought I do in this life, and for what can I hope? Those are the big things of life. What can I really know? I can know God. I can know God personally, and to know him is life eternal. What ought I do with this life? I ought to do the will of God. Above all else, I ought to do the will of God and follow in his steps. For what can I hope? I can hope for eternity with God. Immortality, that's what I can hope for.

Clarence Macartney writes it as good as anybody or better than most people. He says,

> What Jesus taught in the streets of Capernaum, he teaches in 1,000 villages today. What he taught in Jerusalem, he teaches in London and New York. What he taught on the banks of the Jordan and on the shores of the Sea of Galilee, he teaches on the banks of the Thames and the Hudson. As long as the heart has passions, as long

47

as life has woes, the words of Jesus will speak to the soul of men. And so you remember, he told us, "Heaven and earth will pass away. My words will not pass away." You can count on that.[2]

On the isle of Patmos, John had a vision of Jesus Christ. You remember how he gives that in the book of Revelation. And in the midst of the seven golden candlesticks, Jesus Christ is holding the seven stars in his right hand, and his countenance is like the blazing sun, so that John can scarcely look at him. So John falls at his feet as a dead man, and this is what he hears, as Jesus Christ lifted him up and said, "Fear not. I am the first and the last. I am he that liveth and was dead. And behold, I am alive for evermore. Amen. And I have the keys of hell and of death" (Revelation 1:18). Did you hear that? Jesus Christ said, "I have the keys. I hold the keys."

A lot of people are saying, "How can we get out of this mess?" The world is a mess. Remember September 11th, what a turmoil, what a commotion. The whole world was reeling from it. What is the way out? Who has the keys? Who has the answers?

Some say that education is the answer. We know that isn't true. One of the commonly accepted solutions to our problems is to have more schools, and I hear that all the time on television. If we could just educate these people, we'd get this thing all taken care of. More money, more education, more teachers, better training. But for years, we've been pouring money into education, and what do we have? Crime on the increase. Sexual immorality out of control. And the shootings are taking place even in the schools. Education doesn't have the answer. Education has a place, but it doesn't have the keys.

Science doesn't have the keys either. I remember when they first had the atom bomb. I'd never heard of such a thing. I called it the Adam bomb for a long time; I found out only later that it's the atom bomb. The United States had it, and nobody else had it. We were the superpower, and we could do as we wanted. Then they put a man on the moon and he walked around on the moon, and science became the god of many, many people. But science won't work. We see all of the beautiful work of science, the advancement of science, as the towers came crashing down by these super jets that the scientists have made. We saw it all at work, and what did it bring? Death and destruction.

World statesmen, the diplomats—they say they have the answer. So they go to the United Nations, but they lock out Jesus. Jesus Christ is the key. They'll never find peace and they'll never solve the world's situation until they get the only keys—Jesus Christ, the Son of God. Only Jesus has the keys. He says, "I am he that liveth and was dead. And behold, I have the keys." You see, he *is* the key.

You see it played out, for instance, in the life of Todd and Lisa Beamer. On September 11, 2001, Todd was on Flight 93, and many believe that it was planned to strike the U.S. Capitol building in Washington and destroy it. What would have happened if that had taken place? Todd Beamer was on that plane, and because of his bravery and the bravery of a lot of others with him, the attack was aborted, and the plane crashed in a field in Pennsylvania.[3]

So Lisa Beamer now stands with her faith, true to God, trusting God, and witnessing. *Newsweek* magazine had an article[4] that called Lisa a national icon. And so she is, because she had that faith in Christ. In the time when everything was collapsing, she stood true to the Lord and loved the Lord and witnessed for Christ. She stands as a beautiful demonstration of faith in the Lord Jesus Christ. She released a book entitled, *Let's Roll!*—the words of her husband as they made a counterattack on their hijackers. In this book she writes, "In fact, you're a sinner and you deserve only death. The fact that God has offered you hope of eternal life is amazing. You should be overwhelmed with joy and gratitude."

Lisa Beamer knew what it was to suffer loss before the loss of her husband. She lost her father when she was fifteen years old, and she became angry with God. The Newsweek article tells about how she seethed because she was angry toward God. She says, "We had a Norman Rockwell home in upper New York. It was beautiful, the ideal model home." But her dad was taken when she was a teenager, and she was angry with God. She stayed angry with God until she got into a church, and a counselor at a Christian college talked to her. In her story, the counselor tells her, more or less, to get over it and accept that God had allowed her father to die for a reason. She did get over it. As hard as it was, and as difficult as it was, she looked beyond that and loved her God.

In her book,[5] Lisa talks about "that experience of losing my dad, fifteen years old, being angry with God and wondering why, demanding answers…" She got through it, and she put it in her past, and she went with God. She writes that this experience has helped her understand how Todd's untimely death has a purpose known to God, though not yet known to her. She doesn't know, but God knows, and she shines like a beautiful star, a witness to the grace of God. Lisa Beamer went on to testify of her faith in Jesus Christ. Programs like *Good Morning America*, *The Today Show*, *Dateline*, *20/20*, *60 Minutes*, *Oprah*, and others clamored to share her story, and she was able to be a witness for Jesus Christ.

On one of her television interviews on a national television program, a group of Russian reporters were greatly impressed by that woman's testimony and her faith in God and in Jesus Christ. They flew over to speak with her themselves, and they asked for a private interview, which she granted. Lisa Beamer invited the Russians into the Princeton Alliance Church in New Jersey, and she took them to the room where Todd Beamer used to teach Sunday school. On the board was a diagram, and on this diagram there was a picture depicting the chasm between a sinless God and a sinful people—the righteousness of God and a sinful people. There was a cross between that chasm, between a sinful people and a righteous God. The bridge over that chasm was the cross of Christ on which the Savior died.

These Russians looked at that, and a man named Eugene—a Russian bureau chief—said that he'd never seen anything like that, and he asked her to explain it. She explained it to them, and he committed his life to Christ. He went back to Russia, and he had a national television program on which he told about Lisa Beamer and he gave the diagram of a sinless God and a sinful people and the cross of Jesus Christ, and it went on national television in Russia. Lisa Beamer began to think of those beautiful words of Joseph to his brothers in Genesis: "You intended to harm me, but God intended it for good, to accomplish what is now being done, the saving of many lives."

Jesus Christ is the key. There's nowhere else to go. There's nowhere else to look. You have to come to him. Oh, that America would come to God! If America would just take that key. That's the only way out of our struggles, I'm sure.

And so, Jesus Christ then finally becomes the eternal Redeemer. Yesterday, he was on that cross, suffering for the sins of the world. Today, he is offering that cross and that salvation to you.

Tomorrow—what will be tomorrow? Well, the apostle John had a vision of that too, and he gets a glimpse of heaven, and he gets to hear for a moment the music as they're singing up in heaven. John says, "The singing floats down to earth and it's like a great choir." He says, "I can hear what they're singing." John says, "They are singing unto him that loved us and washed us from our sins in his own blood—unto him be glory and dominion forever and ever." They're singing about the cross of Christ, Jesus Christ, who made redemption possible for all of us.

How about your yesterdays? Have you got any skeletons in the closet? Got any sins, any failures, mistakes? Got any transgressions? Are there some things that you'd like to have blotted out and taken away? Is there an abortion in your past? Get to Christ, and get cleansing from that sin.

Oh, America. How America needs to repent! We want the Taliban to repent, and we want everybody else to repent, but America needs to repent over our millions of abortions, and this partial-birth abortion, which is beastly. You think God's going to turn his head away from America and say, "God bless America"? We need to repent. Don't worry about those other nations and the terrorists and all. America needs to get right with God.

If there are those things in your past, listen to what God says: "Their sins and iniquities will I remember no more. As far as the east is from the west, so far hath he removed our transgressions from us. Though your sins be as scarlet, they shall be as white as snow. Though they be red like crimson, they shall be as wool." How about your yesterday?

How is it with you today? How are you getting along today? Do you have some fears? Do you have burdens or sorrows or disappointments? Is there loneliness in your life? Do you have infirmities or longings or temptations? Is there a thorn in the flesh? How are things with you today? Well, today Jesus is saying, "Cast thy burden upon the Lord." He is saying, "Come unto me all ye that are weary and heavy laden, and I'll give you rest."

He is here today. No pie in the sky stuff here. This is real and this is literal, and it works in the lives of people. If you come to Jesus Christ, you can find remission and you can find help. He's right here to help you right now. He's real, and he's here right in your room where you're reading, right at your sick bed or your wheelchair. He's there with you in your prison cell. He's there as you travel or as you feed the livestock. Remember what the psalmist said? "God is a very present help in time of trouble." Have you got troubles? Get to Jesus. Not yesterday, but today. You have today.

What about tomorrow? Jesus is the same forever. Christ is there for your tomorrow. If you just come to him, he'll be there. Some day, when you come to the last day and the last step of your trip, and you come to the valley of the shadow of death, and if Jesus has not yet returned, then every last one of us are going to end there. Just because you're young doesn't mean that you might not be there. I recently buried a young man not forty years old, maybe thirty-five. He should've had another fifty years. As the Germans say, "The old must go, but the young can go."

Are you right with God? You ought to be right with God. Tomorrow is hidden from us, and yet we don't fear, because he's the same yesterday and today and forever, and I know how loving and kind and forgiving he is.

I know how many times he has helped me when I've failed. When I get done with a sermon, I sometimes think, "What a mess." Or, "Why did I say that? Why didn't I say it differently?" But you know what I do? I just say, "Lord, you've got to cover for me." And I go home and I eat dinner. Yep. I eat all the more. And I cook up another next Sunday, and blunder through and tell the Lord, "You knew what a mess I'd be before you ever called me, but you called me so I'll blunder along." He covers me.

He's the same today, he's the same tomorrow. He'll take care of me tomorrow, and I don't know what a day may bring forth. It may bring the valley of the shadow of death for me, but I can tell you this: I don't have to worry a bit, because he's there all the way. That's what the psalmist said when he talked about death, and he said, "Yea, though I walk through the valley of the shadow of death, I will fear no evil." He says, "I'm not afraid to die. I will fear no evil." Why? Because Lord, you're with me. You're with me—not because I've been good, not because I have money, not because I have friends, not because I have influence—but because I have Jesus. I have the key. I have the Savior. I have the Redeemer.

Will you trust Jesus as your Savior? Have you personally asked him into your heart? Have you openly and unashamedly confessed him before others? Have you taken your stand for Christ? And if you have, are you living for him? Are you committed to him? Are you honoring him in your life? Are you trying to serve him? We all fail but he knows our heart, and he knows if we really want to do business. He knows if we really love him. He's there tomorrow, and he'll walk with us and he'll help us. Just accept Christ, trust Christ, and serve Christ.

Dear heavenly Father, we do thank you for the wonderful Savior, Jesus our Lord. We thank you that he loves us. But oh, God, you're the God of judgment, and if we die in our sins, have mercy on our soul. May there be many who will put their faith in you today. In Jesus's name, amen.

JESUS
MY FRIEND

John 15:7-14

If you abide in Me, and My words abide in you, you will ask what you desire, and it shall be done for you. By this My Father is glorified, that you bear much fruit; so you will be My disciples.

As the Father loved Me, I also have loved you; abide in My love. If you keep My commandments, you will abide in My love, just as I have kept My Father's commandments and abide in His love.

These things I have spoken to you, that My joy may remain in you, and that your joy may be full. This is My commandment, that you love one another as I have loved you. Greater love has no one than this, than to lay down one's life for his friends. You are My friends if you do whatever I command you.

LET'S TALK NOW ABOUT TRUSTING JESUS, SWEET JESUS, because he's a friend.

Solomon talked about Jesus. Jesus hadn't been born yet, but Solomon writes about God, and this God comes in the form of Jesus. Solomon was a man of great wisdom, and here's what he says about Jesus "He that maketh many friends doeth it to his own destruction; but there is a friend that sticketh closer than a brother" (Proverbs 18:24).

So, everybody wants to have a friend. There isn't any question about that. We need friends, and we want friends. Man doesn't live totally alone. He has longings for associations with other people. We thank God when we have friends, but we ought to be very careful with a great crowd of acquaintances, that they don't come too close. That is, be very careful who you take in as a friend. A close friend should be somebody you can confide in, someone that you can open up your heart to.

There aren't many people who you can do that with. We ought to, in Christ's name, be good to all and help all along the way that we can, but we can't help everybody. We can never really be as close to some as we are to others. Again, we ought to have close friends. But if you have two or three close friends, you're very fortunate. In fact, if you have even one close friend, you're very fortunate.

So God talks to us today. He tells us that there's a friend you can have that's closer than a brother, that's closer than any person on earth.

He's a friend who will never leave you or forsake you. He is the friend that Solomon talked about.

Solomon said this long ago, and he was thinking of a friend that's above the human level. The preacher of old was talking about the greatest friend in all the world. That friend who Solomon wrote about was Jesus Christ. Now, he didn't know him yet. Jesus had yet to come, but now we know him.

It is sweet to trust in Jesus. That's our friend. We can trust in him and rely upon him. I'm here to tell you today that I know this wonderful friend. I know him personally. I know him intimately. I don't know him fully, or everything about him. But I remember that Jesus said, "I no longer call you servants. I now call you friends" (John 15:15).

I've walked with this friend for ninety years. Knowing him has changed my life. I often wonder where I would be today, what would have happened to me, if I hadn't had this wonderful friend that I found nine decades ago. So, out of experience, I want to tell you about this friend, this wonderful, wonderful friend, Jesus Christ the Savior.

I want to say first of all that this wonderful friend of mine loves me. I guess that was the first thing that drew me to him. I knew that he loved me. I remember an evangelist preaching one night in my country school, an evangelist from the Christian and Missionary Alliance. He came to our country school and he preached. I remember he told about the Good Samaritan and how a man was robbed and left with nothing but dirty clothes. But along came the Good Samaritan, who loved him and helped him. If we come to the one who loves us, Jesus will change us and he'll cleanse us and he'll give us new clothes.

There are a lot of things in the Bible I just never understood, but I can understand that God loves me. I know that God is good. I know that God is holy. I know that God is pure. I know that God is matchless in his sinlessness. I know that this wonderful God is beautiful in every way. Let me tell you something else I know; I know this Jesus Christ loves me. He loves me in spite of my failure, in spite of my pollution, in spite of the way I've sinned. He is the one who loves me.

He told me that he loves me. He told me that in the Bible, in John 3:16, when he said, "God so loved the world..." That's me. I'm part of his world. I'm glad he didn't put in my name— "God so loved Harold Salem"—because I found out that there are some other Harold Salems living right now. I think they're very fortunate to have a nice name like that. But if an angel said out of heaven, "God loves Harold Salem," then which Harold Salem did he love? But when he said, "God so loved the world," and that "whosoever" believes in his Son Jesus will not perish but have everlasting life—then I'm in. I know he loves me.

You know something else? He not only told me that he loved me, but he demonstrated it, he proved it. There are people who say they love us, but they don't treat us right. They never do anything to help us or show that love. They don't really love us. If you really love somebody, you're going to give them love. You're going to do something for them. You just can't help it.

This friend of mine, Jesus, not only told me that he loved me, but he demonstrated it. He showed me. It's there for instance in Romans 5:8, where Paul says, "God commendeth his love toward us, in that, while we were yet sinners, Christ died for us." That's how much he loves you. That's how much he loves me. He loved us enough to die for us. Jesus said in John 15:13, "Greater love has no man than this, that a man lay down his life for his friends." There are very few on the human level who have anybody that would die for them, lay down their life for them. If you have a friend who would die for you, you are very fortunate. Very few have.

When the rubber meets the road, I'm not so sure how many would die for another person. But Jesus did. He died for me, if you can imagine, while I was a sinner. I was a rebel against God. I was against God. I was on the devil's team. But he died for me. In those days of my life, I lived for myself. I lived against him. I wasn't for him. I wasn't on his team. This wonderful friend not only tells me that he loves me, but he came and he died for me when I was his enemy. He demonstrated, and he proved it.

Because he loves me, he's always faithful to me. He's always true to me. He's always tender to me. He's always strong for me. He always helps me. He's always generous with me. Think of that for a minute. He's always faithful.

Over the years, he's never deserted me a single time. I've been like Peter. I've denied the Lord when I should have spoken up. But for ninety years, there's never been a single time when he ever forsook me. I was unfaithful to him, but he was faithful to me. I've had others forsake me. I've had others desert me. I've had people who were my friends for fifty years who turned on me. I know what it's like to get stabbed in the back. But with the Lord Jesus, though I was unfaithful to him, he was never unfaithful to me.

There's one Savior. There's one friend, my blessed Savior, who never deserts me. I can always count on him. He never gets tired of me. He's never turned his back on me. Yes, I have forgotten him, but he hasn't forgotten me.

Do you remember when Jesus finished his work on the cross, and then he was buried? And on the third day, he was raised. Then he walked among men for many days. And then he was going to leave, for his work on earth was done, so he called his disciples together. He gave them a commission to go into all the world and preach the gospel. That's what we're supposed to do. That's what we're doing through the *Christian Worship Hour* and these books.

When he was all done with his work, this wonderful Savior gave us the Great Commission. And then they went out of the city of Jerusalem and went up on the Mount of Olives, and Jesus said, "I'm going to leave you now." He ascended up into heaven.

I can imagine how they looked at him as he went up into heaven. They said, "Finally, the clouds, the clouds of glory." Maybe it's the glory he laid aside when he came to earth as a baby. A cloud of glory took him in, and they saw him no more. The disciples might have said, "Will he ever remember us? When he goes to heaven, will he ever think about us? He is so rich now. He's so wonderful now. Will he ever remember us?" Sometimes friends don't remember us.

You remember about Joseph, when he was in prison—he made two friends, a butler and a baker. One of them got freed. The butler was going to go free. Joseph said to that butler, "Remember me." But the Bible says, "The butler forgot Joseph." He forgot all about him. I've had someone forget me. I'm sure you have too.

So here's Jesus about to go up into heaven. His disciples are thinking, "Will he forget us? Will he remember us?" How their hearts must have yearned as they saw the dearest on earth ascend up into heaven. They didn't think he was going to do that. They thought he was the Messiah who would break the chains of Rome. They thought he was going to set up his kingdom right then, but that's yet to come. They didn't know that.

As he was going up into heaven, they were thinking, What are we going to do? Well, they didn't have to wonder very long, did they? Two men in dazzling white stood beside them. These angels came, dazzling white angels, and they said, "Ye men of Galilee, why stand ye looking up into heaven? This same Jesus, which was received up from you into heaven, shall so come in like manner as you behold him go into heaven" (Acts 1:11). This friend had left them, but the moment he was out of their sight, he was thinking of them. The moment he was out of sight, he got those angels, and he said, "Go tell my friends that they don't have to worry. I'm going to come back, and not as a spirit. I'm going to come back in the flesh, my immortal flesh."

By the way, when he comes, he's going to put his feet on Mount Moriah and the whole world is going to see him. The whole world is going to kneel down and say that he's the Son of God. Boy, that's going to be a hard kneel for the people who are now cursing God and defying God. But they're going to bow their head and say, "Jesus Christ is God." You better bow now while you've got a chance.

He never forgot them for a minute. He could have forgotten his friends, because when he entered into heaven, there was dazzling light, there was glory. The glory of God shone upon him as on the Mount of Transfiguration.

With this, a multitude of angels were there—thousands upon thousands, millions of them, all singing his praises. The seraphim were there, and the cherubim were there. The redeemed from ages past were there. There was shouting and the glory of the praise, and the angelic singing of the realms on high, and all the tumult and rejoicing of redemption—but Jesus thought about his disciples, his friends down on earth. He sent them the messengers.

No, sir, my friend never forgets me. He loves me, and he helps me.

Sometimes I think, "Oh, he's forgotten all about me." I'm praying for these things, and nothing happens. I don't feel him, and I don't see him. I think he forgets me. But when I'm sober and when I'm honest and when I'm sincere, I know that he's there. I know he hasn't forgotten me. I know he hears my cry. I know he's with me. I know he's as close as my breath.

I'm his friend. Just think of it. He takes pleasure in me, because he loves me with all his heart. That's the way he loves you. He doesn't have favorites. He's not a respecter of persons. He loves you with all his heart. You're on his heart, and he knows your name. He knows every time you shed a tear. Oh, he is so wonderful!

You know something else about this wonderful Savior? He's my advocate in heaven. He's my great High Priest. Satan finds fault with me all the time. I sin every day. I'm not proud of it. Well, you say, "What sins do you do?" Well, wouldn't you like to know. I confess them unto Jesus so you'll never know. So, forget it.

But I sin every day. I don't know about you, but I know I do. Satan is there. He has a fine-tooth comb. When he can find any little thing, he takes it to the throne in heaven and says, "Look at what your friend down there is doing. Look at what he said. Look at what he thought." And then Jesus intercedes for me. He's my lawyer up in heaven. He's my friend, and he helps me.

What a wonderful, wonderful Savior! My friend is always true to me. Sometimes he rebukes me. Yes, he does. It's not out loud, but down in my heart. "Harold, you shouldn't have done that. You should have done this. You should have helped this person. You shouldn't have thought that way. You shouldn't have had that attitude." When he talks to me, sometimes I don't always like it. Sometimes I try to get around it. Sometimes I try to make excuses. Sometimes I try to evade it. Sometimes I try to explain it away. But he's my friend. He won't give up, and he just keeps punching.

He's like physical therapists, when they work on a muscle. I was in therapy the other day, and this woman got to work on some muscle. I thought, "She's going to kill me." Boy, she just kept boring in there. The hardest place she pushed was on the sore spots. That's what I was paying her for. Well, that's what Jesus does. When there's something wrong in our heart, he won't make friends with it. He won't accept it. He won't compromise. He knows exactly what I'm thinking.

Sometimes he's pretty blunt, and he'll tell you when you're off base. He'll tell me when I'm off base, just as he did with Peter. Jesus was preaching and teaching, and a lot of people were leaving him. Jesus speaks to his disciples about how he's going to have to suffer and how he's going to die for them. But Peter says, "No, you're not going to die. We're not going to let you die." You know what Jesus said to Peter? He said, "Get thee behind me, Satan." That's what he said to Peter.

So Jesus is blunt. He's going to tell us when we're off base. I thank God that he does this, because otherwise I wouldn't find my way back. I'm blind and dumb and stupid. I could be sinning and never ever know it. I could be going way off base and say, " No, Jesus, you're not going to

die." Jesus says, "Listen, Harold, get you behind me, Satan. You're thinking the way the devil is thinking." But Jesus, this wonderful Savior, is
tender and he always does it in love.

The Bible talks about the potter with his clay and how the potter
forms it. Sometimes it hurts when he forms that clay. He's trying to
make something out of you, friend. That hurts because we're living clay,
you see, but he's trying to make something. So that's what he's doing
with Peter. "Peter, you're off base. You're taking Satan's point of view."
So he reproves Peter. That's a mark of real friendship. The fake friends,
they'll just butter you up and flatter you. Flattery is like perfume. Smell
it, don't swallow it. But Jesus doesn't flatter us. He tells us what the score
is.

In the old hymn "In the Secret of His Presence," Ellen L. Goreh
penned these words:

Do you think He ne'er reproves me?
What a false friend He would be
if He never, never told me
of the sins which He must see.

Real friends level with us. Jesus levels with us. Not only when I'm wrong,
but when I'm right, he praises me. There are a lot of people who think
they're never going to hear Jesus say "Well done, good and faithful servant" until they die, when they stand before the judgment seat of Christ.
Well, you're wrong, because he can say that whenever you give your best
for him. You've been in a struggle for him, and you didn't yield to temptation, and he says, "Well done, good and faithful servant." When you've
witnessed for him, and you may think you've done a poor job of it, but
then he'll come to you and say, "Well done, good and faithful servant."

Yes, when the battle is won, but I've been wounded in the battle, he will say, "Well done, good and faithful servant." I guess it's the "well done" whispered at the close of the day that gives me strength for tomorrow, but he's always honest with me. God is a friend. Jesus is a friend. He rebukes me in my wandering, and he praises me in my victories. He's a friend and he's so tender.

Beyond all words, in my sorrows, he's sympathetic. We've all had sorrows, or will have. You don't live long in this world without sorrows. Satan sees to it that there's sin in the world. But we may have to bear our sorrows all alone, unless we have this friend. But I can take it to Jesus, and tell it to Jesus. He's my divine friend.

My friend is tender. He never forsakes me, and he never asks me to carry more than I can bear. Sometimes we say, "These sorrows, these troubles, these trials are too heavy." No, they aren't. You may think they're too heavy, but the Lord Jesus Christ takes care of us and he never gives us too much.

You know what the Scripture says? He bends over us and says, "I have yet many things to say unto you, but you cannot bear them now" (John 16:12).

He says to Peter, "Dear friend, I have some things I want you to know. I have some things I want you to do. I have some things I want to share, but you're not strong enough yet. I'm going to wait until you're strong enough." Did you hear that? He says, "I have yet many things to say unto you, but you cannot bear them now" (John 16:12). So he's waiting. Sometimes he waits years.

I don't know what he has for me to carry, but I know I had to say goodbye to my wife, my dear Beulah. I had to say goodbye to my little granddaughter. Those aren't easy things. But they didn't come until I was ready. Maybe he has more, I don't know. But he's tender, and he understands, and he cares. I love him.

Keep in mind that he's strong. My friend is strong. He's tender, but he's strong. He's stronger than Satan. Satan has the whole world under his wicked sway and power. He's the prince of the power of the air and boy, does he cause problems and troubles in the world. He's a devil, he's a liar, he's a deceiver—but Jesus Christ is greater.

Someday Satan is going to be vanquished. We know how the story ends. Look in the book of Revelation. Satan is cast into the lake of fire, and he never comes back. He comes back out of the bottomless pit for a little time. But when that time is done, he's put into the lake of fire forever and ever and ever. That's exactly where he belongs. And our Lord Jesus Christ is powerful and he's strong. We can rely on him. Someday, we're going to see him in all of his power. Jesus says, "All power is given unto me"—all power in heaven and earth.

Our wonderful Father is generous and he shares that power with me. We sing that old song "A Child of the King" (by Hattie E. Buell), and it begins,

My Father is rich in houses and lands.
He holdeth the wealth of the world in his hands!
Of rubies and diamonds, of silver and gold,
his coffers are full, he has riches untold.

He has everything, and he's generous. Look at all that he gives me—I'm nearly a hundred years old, and I can still preach the glorious gospel of Jesus Christ. When you look at your life, you have to say, "Yes, God is good. Yes, God is kind. Yes, God is generous."

What if he treated us the way we deserve? I'm thankful that he doesn't. I never asked God for justice. I don't want justice. I want mercy. I want grace. This Jesus is so generous.

Yes, he owns the whole world of rubies and diamonds and silver and gold, and his coffers are full of untold riches. You can't measure the wealth and power of Jesus Christ. That's my friend. That's not my enemy. He's my friend.

Because of this wonderful friend, I'm never lonely. I'm never alone. He's always close at hand, because he sticketh closer than a brother.

So I want to ask you today: Are you within the circle of his friends? You need not be left out of that circle, if you don't want to be. Are you?

This friend I talk about will be your friend. He was your friend long before you're his. He longs for your friendship. The advance is on his side, not on ours. He says, "You haven't chosen me—I've chosen you." It's downright amazing that he has chosen us. He tells us in the Scriptures and he's chosen all of us. He's not willing that any should perish. You're all chosen to be his friends—but you won't be his friends until you come to him.

Jesus wants us to be his friends. He says, "You are my friends, if you do the things which I command you." What does he command us? Well, here's one of his commandments: "Come unto me, I'll give you rest." Is that a hard commandment? You better come to Jesus. You need not understand all the mysteries of life. You need not understand all the mysteries of theology, and how it all happens. But this is a friend that sticketh closer than a brother, and he's seeking your friendship.

He wants you to come to him, so he can say, "I no longer call you my servants. I call you my friends." Is he talking to you, dear friend? In your heart, do you yearn to come to Jesus? In your heart, he wants you to hear him say, "Come unto me, all you that are weary and are heavy laden, and I will give you rest. Take my yoke upon you, and learn of me, for I am meek and lowly in heart, and you shall find rest unto your souls. For my yoke is easy, and my burden is light." He's speaking to your heart because he loves you. He wants to be your friend. He wants you to come.

You say, "But how do I come? What do I do?" Well, in your own words, just confess your sins to Jesus. Billy Graham says, "If there's some big sin, name it," or name all of them. Put them in a basket and say, "Here they are Jesus, all of my sins. I'm a sinner"—and confess your sins. Then ask him to come into your heart and to cleanse you, to wash in the blood of the Lamb and take away your sins. He will come into your heart. And the Lord says, "Though your sins be as scarlet, they shall be as white as snow; though they be red like crimson, they're going to be like wool." They're all going to be gone. Then thank him for coming into your heart, and then tell somebody that you accepted Jesus. Be a witness for him.

I really believe in my heart that somewhere, somebody is praying right now:

"Dear Jesus, I'm a sinner. I'm sorry for my sins. I ask you to come into my heart and wash them away in your blood. I'll never see them again. I'll be clean and I'll be pure. I will stand in your righteousness. When I come to heaven's gates, they won't see me; they'll see you. They'll see Jesus, because I'm clothed in your righteousness. I thank you, Jesus. I'm going to serve you the best that I can. And I want to tell those around me what I did." Tell somebody that you accepted Jesus.

If you're a backslider, come on back today to your Lord. Rededicate your life to the Lord. All of you that are weary and heavy laden, lay your head on this dear friend, on his bosom. He'll carry you in his arms like a shepherd carrying the lambs. He loves you, loves you so much that he died for you.

Dear Jesus, thank you for being our Savior. Thank you for all those that you are saving right now, all who are coming to you right now. May all the praise and glory be to you, the great Son of God, Savior of the world, Jesus the Christ. In his name, amen.

PART II

The Miracles of Jesus

HEALING THE PARALYTIC

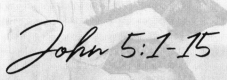

John 5:1-15

After this there was a feast of the Jews, and Jesus went up to Jerusalem. Now there is in Jerusalem by the Sheep Gate a pool, which is called in Hebrew, Bethesda, having five porches. In these lay a great multitude of sick people, blind, lame, paralyzed, waiting for the moving of the water. For an angel went down at a certain time into the pool and stirred up the water; then whoever stepped in first, after the stirring of the water, was made well of whatever disease he had. Now a certain man was there who had an infirmity thirty-eight years. When Jesus saw him lying there, and knew that he already had been in that condition a long time, He said to him, "Do you want to be made well?"

The sick man answered Him, "Sir, I have no man to put me into the pool when the water is stirred up; but while I am coming, another steps down before me."

Jesus said to him, "Rise, take up your bed and walk." And immediately the man was made well, took up his bed, and walked.

And that day was the Sabbath. The Jews therefore said to him who was cured, "It is the Sabbath; it is not lawful for you to carry your bed."

He answered them, "He who made me well said to me, 'Take up your bed and walk.'"

Then they asked him, "Who is the Man who said to you, 'Take up your bed and walk'?" But the one who was healed did not know who it was, for Jesus had withdrawn, a multitude being in that place. Afterward Jesus found him in the temple, and said to him, "See, you have been made well. Sin no more, lest a worse thing come upon you."

The man departed and told the Jews that it was Jesus who had made him well.

When we look at the miracles of Jesus, we find that the first one was his making water into wine at Cana of Galilee. Second was the healing of the nobleman's son. Next we come to his healing of a paralytic in John 5.

We're told in this passage that Jesus went to a feast. We don't know exactly what feast it was. Most Bible teachers think it probably was the Feast of the Passover, but that really doesn't matter. He went to a feast, and that meant that there would be many, many people in that city.

Jesus went to a place called the pool of Bethesda. That's in the northeast corner of the old city of Jerusalem, and the pool is still there today, and you can see it. It's about forty feet below street level because of the additions to the city over time, but the pool is still there if you were to visit.

The name Bethesda means "house of mercy." The pool itself is surrounded by five different porches or porticoes, and on these porches there were multitudes of people—hundreds or maybe thousands of people. John describes them as being impotent, blind, lame, or paralyzed.

Of course that's a picture of the world today, because sin has brought sickness and sorrow and death into this universe. It doesn't mean that when people are really sick, they're really sinful. It just means that it's a part of life. When our parents sinned against God in the garden of Eden, he put a curse on this earth, and it's all over the earth, and part of that curse is sickness and disease and death. That came from our first parents. It's the outworking of sin.

Jesus comes and he sees these people in these various conditions, and he sees one man there who's been paralyzed for thirty-eight years. That's a long time to be in a state of paralysis. He was there because every so often, maybe once a year, an angel would come and there would be a stirring of this pool. We don't know exactly what that was, but there was a moving or a bubbling or something, and the people knew it. And the first one to get into that pool after the stirring by the angel, that person would be healed no matter what the malady might be.

This man has been here for thirty-eight years, and he has not been able to get into the water because of his condition, so he doesn't have a very pleasant prospect. He has been there for thirty-eight years, can you imagine? Maybe came when he was eight or ten years old, I don't know, but all of his life he's been at the pool, and all of his life he hoped that maybe he could get into that pool, but he never was able to do it.

Jesus comes to him and he says to him, "Arise, take up your bed and walk."

In his commentary on this miracle,[6] Marcus Dods says that it's important to notice three things that are implied in Christ's words here, when he says, "Rise, take up thy bed, and walk."

First, when Jesus says "Rise" to this man, it means that he is supposed to do something he cannot do. He cannot stand, but Jesus tells him to rise, and he rises and stands. This is a picture of our salvation. We cannot save ourselves, but if we call on the name of the Lord, we can do something we couldn't do. We can come to Christ and be saved.

Jesus also says, "Take up your bed." When he said for the man to take up his bed, he meant, "Don't leave any ways to fall back. You're not going to stand for a little bit and tremble and fall back. You take up that cot. You're burning your bridges behind you, and you're to make no provision for failure."

Then Jesus tells the man, "Walk." He was saying, "Don't be carried. Don't be a baby all your life. Get going and do something for God." The man is healed, and this all takes place, and the man rejoices because he's healed by the power of Jesus Christ.

Now, I want you to look at three things in this story. The first thing we have—and when you really think about it and reflect upon it, it'll come to you as clear as a bell—Jesus didn't heal everybody there. As a matter of fact, he healed only one. There were hundreds or thousands there, and he heals one. Now, what do you make of that? Why would Jesus heal only one person?

Then we're told in the Scriptures after he healed that one person, Jesus withdrew. The *New International Version* has it he "slipped away." Jesus healed that one, and when all those people saw him heal that one person, you can imagine the clamor among them all. Everybody would want to be healed. Who wouldn't want to be healed? But Jesus heals just one person, and he slips away.

I want to ask you something. Have you ever wondered why Jesus didn't heal everybody at the pool of Bethesda while he was there, and while he was at it? He sure had the power. That was no problem for Jesus, because God can do anything. Never limit God. I hear people limiting God. "Oh, we'd like to do this, but we don't have enough money. We would like to do that, but we can't do that"—and they put bounds on

God. But if God calls us to do something, we can do it, whether it involves money, or walking, or witnessing, or breaking habits, or anything else. We can do it, if we want to do it, and his will is that we do it.

Jesus didn't heal everybody. So why didn't he heal everybody? He didn't heal everybody then, and he doesn't heal everybody now. How come? What goes here?

Well, the apostle Paul is a good example of that. He says, "I was given a sickness which has been a thorn in my flesh. Three different times, I begged God to make me well again, and each time he said no. Each time he says, 'No, but I am with you. That's all you need. My power shows up most in the weak people.'" The great and mighty Paul, who did so much for Christ, who was truly one of his saints, was not going to be healed.

We see that also in the Old Testament—with Elisha, for instance. Elisha had fallen sick with the sickness of which he died. Daniel talks also about being ill and sick.

And we have Timothy's story in the New Testament. Here was a young man with some kind of infirmity, some kind of an ailment of the stomach. And Paul says, "Take a little wine for your stomach's sake." In other words, he tells him to use wine for medicinal purposes—not to drink it and drown in it. But we have medicine now. We don't need to be taking that wine. But instead of Paul healing Timothy, instead of Paul sending him a blessed handkerchief or something like that, Paul says, "I can't heal you, Timothy, so take a little wine to compensate for this."

Another story is that of Epaphroditus, who was sick nigh unto death. Paul mentions also a good servant of God named Trophimus, and he says, "I left him at Miletum, because he was sick."

God just doesn't heal everybody. Sometimes he says yes, and sometimes he says no, but it is always in love and understanding, and it is always with this backdrop for the child of God: that all things work together for good to those who love the Lord. Every time that he presses on us and moves us to bring some hard thing into our life, it's always with his nail-pierced pain, and with loving, kind hands.

Jesus is saying here, "I haven't come to heal the whole world. I've come to save a soul. I've come to save this man's soul." I want you to see him saying, "Of all these people here, of all the needs that are here, the need that's greatest is the soul, because I can heal all your bodies and you can live a few years but then die and go to hell. What good is that? But if you have that wonderful salvation and the healing of the soul, you'll live forever."

I read the story of the plane crashing into the towers of the World Trade Center. We read about how in that mountain of rubble that was left, they looked for any survivors. In kind of a madness of effort, they immediately worked to see if there were any survivors.

But there was something there under that pile of debris that few people talked about. There in an underground vault, there were twelve tons of pure gold. It was held there by Comex metals trading division of the New York Mercantile Exchange.[7] But when those towers collapsed, were the rescuers looking for the gold? No, they were looking for human beings.

That's what Jesus is saying. That body is so important, but there's something more important than the body—that precious soul that will never, ever, ever die. It will be forever in heaven, or it will be forever in hell. Jesus is saying he could've healed every one of the people there, but he was going to heal only one, in order to give this message, especially to the Pharisees and the chief priests.

By the way, this happened about the end of the first year of our Lord's ministry, and he healed on the Sabbath, and the Jews never forgave him for that, and they never rested until they had him on the cross. That was the start.

But he was telling us that although the body is precious, the soul is so much more precious.

Pastor Adrian Rogers makes a good comment on this passage:

> If Jesus were interested in being a great healer, he would have gone from person to person and healed them all. But he healed just one man because it was teaching a great spiritual truth of which the healing was a symbol. Jesus didn't come to be the great healer. He came to be the great Savior.[8]

For this man in Bethesda, the big thing was not his body. The big thing was his soul, and that's why Jesus said, "Fear not them which kill the body but are not able to kill the soul, but rather fear him which is able to destroy both soul and body in hell." He's saying that the most important thing about you is your soul inside.

When you die, that soul continues to live on in either heaven or hell. The body is here, but that spirit and soul go to be over there. If you know Jesus, your soul goes to be with God, and he'll raise up that body someday, and that body will be with you in heaven. You'll not only have a soul, you'll have an immortal body as well. If you don't know Jesus Christ, your body is going to be raised up, but only so you can stand in that body at the judgment of the great white throne, from which there's no reprieve and no help, but only eternal crisis—eternal hell for your soul and body.

That's what Jesus is saying. "I could heal the whole world, but what good will that do if that soul isn't saved?"

Then we look at this story in John 5 and we ask a question: Does everybody want to be healed? Jesus had a kind of a strange question. He says, "Wilt thou be made whole? Do you want to get well?" At first blush, it sounds like that's kind of a stupid question.

Look at what the paralytic answers. He says, "Sir, I have no man when the water is troubled to put me into the pool. But while I'm coming, another steppeth down before me." Why doesn't this guy say, "Dear Jesus, I am a mess, and yes, I want you to help me"?

No, he makes excuses, doesn't he? He's telling Jesus why he isn't healed, as though the healing depended on that man himself.

See, that's the problem. You talk to people today, and we want them to come to Christ, but they say, "I will do it myself. I'll get in the pool by myself. I do enough good works so that I can get by all right when the judgment comes."

I saw this from one of the main speakers on a CNN program. The journalist was very incensed toward a pastor he was interviewing, a pastor who was president of a Southern Baptist seminary. This pastor told the journalist that you had to receive Jesus Christ to be saved, and the journalist was incensed at this, because he lived a good life. Now, he isn't the only one. If you go out and talk about this with ten people, nine out of ten will think they're going to heaven because they're doing good work.

We're taught that it's all within ourselves. We're trained that way. We don't need God. Everything we need is within ourselves. We pull up ourselves by our own bootstraps, and we'll do this thing.

That's what this fellow at the pool was saying. He says, "I would get healed, but I can't do it. I can't get there to the pool in time." He was looking at himself, and instead he should have said to Jesus, "I am a lost soul, and I need your salvation."

That's what everybody needs to say. So many people are counting on their works, and yet God says, "For by grace are you saved through faith, and that not of yourselves; it is the gift of God, not of works, lest any man should boast" (Ephesians 2:8-9). Not by works. "But to him that worketh not but believeth on him, that belief is counted for righteousness" (Romans 4:5).

When Jesus asks, "Do you want to be made whole?" we have to cry out and say, "Jesus, I am a poor lost sinner, and I cannot save myself, and I cannot put myself into that pool. I am paralyzed. I am impotent. I am blind. I am naked. I have nothing. Nothing in my hands I bring, simply to thy cross I cling."

There's too much human pride that keeps too many people away. They're too proud to come to Jesus with their honest need. They're too proud to walk forward in a church service and say, "I need the Savior. I need Christ." They're afraid of what people might say. People around town might talk about them.

But you need help. Jesus has paid for all of those sins, but you have to come to him. If you don't come to him, it doesn't do any good.

Sometimes you hear people say, "Well, Jesus paid for the sins of the world. They're all paid. We don't need to worry." Now, that's a half truth. Jesus did pay for the sins of the world. They're all paid, but it won't do you any good unless you personally receive Jesus Christ. You have to receive Christ before that pardon works.

There's an interesting story about a man named George Wilson. In 1829, he was sentenced to be hanged by the state of Pennsylvania for mail robbery and murder. He was in prison after being convicted and sentenced to die, but before he could be put to death, President Andrew Jackson pardoned him. The presidential pardon was sent to the governor of Pennsylvania. The governor sent it to the warden of the prison, and they took the message to George Wilson, and they were amazed when George Wilson said, "I don't want any pardon. I refuse it."

Now they had a problem. He was pardoned, but he wouldn't accept it. The warden couldn't just push him out the doors. What would they do? Well, there was kind of a legal tangle, and it ended up in the U.S. Supreme Court. Chief Justice John Marshall, in rendering the court's decision, said that a pardon is a piece of paper, the value of which depends on its acceptance by the person implicated. If it's refused, it's not a pardon. As a result, George Wilson stayed imprisoned.[9]

I'm going to tell you something. Jesus, when he suffered on that cross, paid for the sins of the world, and he paid for your sins and my sins, and he will pardon them. But you've got to accept that pardon. You've got to humble yourself and say, "I can't do it myself. I'm worthy of death. I'm worthy of hell. I'm a sinner."

Maybe you're a big sinner. Maybe you've only got a little sin. It doesn't make any difference. God says, "If you offend in one point, you're guilty of all the law." We've all broken all the commandments in one way or another, and you've got to admit that and ask him to save you. Then you get the pardon.

Then if this Jesus doesn't heal everybody, if God doesn't heal everybody, I want to come back to that in closing and just say this. What do we do in the light of this? We know it's true that God doesn't heal everybody, and so when I get sick, do I pray for healing? If I have to go to the hospital, do I pray for healing, that God will help me?

Well, I'm going to tell you something, friend. If you get sick and you don't pray for healing, you must be nuts. Of course we pray for healing. We also pray for the souls of our loved ones as well as for their healing. I've prayed for healing and help many times, and God has been good to me, but maybe one of these times I'll pray and I won't get that healing. But we have to pray. If we get sick, we pray.

If God healed every sickness, every time we got sick, if he healed us perfectly, we'd never die unless we had some kind of an accident, so that has to come. But we pray. Of course we pray. But here's the key. We always pray, "Thy will be done."

Pray for healing for yourself. Pray for your friends and your loved ones. When somebody has asked you to pray, write it down. Sometimes we say, "Yeah, I'll pray for you," but we don't pray for them. We should pray for them, but always pray, "Thy will be done on earth as it is in heaven."

That's what the apostle Paul did. He prayed to God for healing, but he wasn't healed. So he continued to pray for healing until God told him very plainly, "Paul, I don't want you to pray that anymore. You're not going to be healed. You're going to have that thorn in the flesh. But my grace is sufficient for you, and my greatness is made great through your weakness. And the weaker you are, the more I can do with you. And the greater I will be, the weaker you are—and so you're going to keep that."

What does Paul do? Did he mope around? Did he go around crying like a baby? Did he feel sorry for himself? Did he feel that he was being shortchanged by God? Did he go back to God and say, "Well, God, I've done so much for you. Can't you do this for me?"

Look at what Paul says he did for God. He says, "I've served God far more than these other people." He says, "I've worked harder, been put in jail oftener. I've been whipped times without number. I've faced death again and again and again. Five different times the Jews gave me their terrible thirty-nine lashes. Three times I was beaten with rods. Once I was stoned. Three times I was shipwrecked. Once I was in the open sea all night and the whole next day. I've traveled many weary miles. I've often been in great danger from flooded rivers, from robbers, from my own people, the Jews, and from the hands of the Gentiles. I've faced grave danger from the mobs in the cities, from the desert and in the stormy seas, from men who claimed to be brothers in Christ but are not. I've lived with weariness and pain and sleepless nights."

And he says, "Often I've been hungry and thirsty and gone without food. Often I had to shiver with cold, without enough clothing to keep me warm. I've had the constant worry of the churches, how they're getting along."

And so now Paul gets sick, and with all of that behind him, he says, "Now, God, would you heal me?" But God says no.

If he'd been like a lot of people I know, they'd just say, "Well, you were a fine God. Look what I did for you, and you won't take this miserable thorn out of my flesh. I'm done with you, God." I've seen that happen. I can still see a woman fifty years ago or so who said she would never go to church and she'd never give God a nickel, because they lost their farm in the Depression. I have a suspicion they probably were lousy farmers, but I don't know. I shouldn't say that, because we lost our farm, and I think we were good farmers. We must wait till we get to heaven to know more about that.

But Paul says, "I've done all these things. I've poured out my whole life for you, God," and God says, "Paul, I'm not going to heal you." Look at what Paul says. "Three different times I begged God to make me well again. Each time he said, 'No, but I am with you. That's all you need. My power shows best in weak people.' So now I'm glad to boast about how weak I am. I'm glad to be able to be a demonstration of Christ's power, instead of showing off my own power and my abilities."

So how do you handle that? You handle that by praying to God, and asking him, and begging him if you want to, however you want to put it—but always close every prayer with this: "Thy will be done on earth as it is in heaven."

Remember when Jesus was in the garden of Gethsemane, and already the cross was starting to cast this big shadow across him. The next day, he was going to be crucified. That was all coming to pass. Jesus in the garden of Gethsemane says, "O my Father, if it be possible, let this cup pass from me. Let this cup pass from me." This is like saying, "O God, take this sickness away from me. O God take this cancer out of my body. O God, I have these troubles and these trials. My mind isn't working right. Something's wrong—and so, O God, heal me." That's what Jesus is saying. "That cross over there—is there any way around that cross?"

After he got done with his prayer, here's how he closed his prayer. "Nevertheless," after all these requests, "Nevertheless, not as I will but as thou wilt." So we pray, "Dear Jesus, please remove this illness," and then we pray, "Not my will, but thine by done." We pray, "Thy will be done on earth as it is in heaven."

Again, Adrian Rogers comments:

Remember that the purpose of miracles in the gospel of John is to teach us greater spiritual lessons and to point us to Jesus. John didn't write the gospel so that paralyzed people might be healed. He wrote it so that lost people might be saved and have abundant life. He wrote it that we might receive strength from above so that by believing in Jesus we can walk in vitality, liberty, and victory day by day.

My dear friend, if you're not a Christian today, I just hope that you will pray for healing. Maybe you do need bodily healing. Pray for it, but pray first of all that God will make you whole spiritually. You're never whole until you're spiritually right with God. Pray that. If you're a Christian, you just pray that also, and pray that God would just help us to receive what he gives us, what he puts in our lives.

Some of the greatest hymns we have are ones that people wrote in great duress, great suffering, great loss—loss of loved ones, loss of health, loss of sight, loss of family. Out of that terrible crushing of that terrible winepress comes this wonderful, beautiful hymn that we sing over and over and over again.

There's a purpose for it all. There's a reason for it all. Jesus suffered for a reason. You and I might suffer for a reason. Oh, we have so many sick people, and we've got some in the hospital. I've talked to them, and I know they want healing, and they want help, and I want it for them, and I pray that they'll have it. I pray to God they'll have it. But I pray more than all else that Jesus will have his way—that the soul will be right, and God will have his way.

We sing it like this in the old hymn "Trusting Jesus" (by Edgar Page):

Simply trusting every day,
trusting through a stormy wave.
Even when my faith is small,
trusting Jesus, that is all.
Brightly doth his Spirit shine
into this poor heart of mine.
While he leads, I cannot fall.
Trusting Jesus, that is all.
Singing if my way is clear,
praying if the path be drear.
If in danger, for him call.
Trusting Jesus, that is all.
Trusting him while life shall last,
trusting him till earth be past,
till within the jasper wall,
trusting Jesus, that is all.
Trusting as the moments fly,
trusting as the days go by,
trusting him whate'er befall.
Trusting Jesus, that's all.

Heavenly Father, we can trust you. We don't have to be afraid to put ourselves in your hands. They're loving hands. They're caring hands. They're hands of wisdom. It's a joy to submit to you. Whatever you have for us in this life, may we gladly receive it and accept it, and if it's some sickness or illness, may we hold it up, hold it up like a banner and say, "This Christ helps me through every battle and every struggle." Thank you for Jesus, wonderful, wonderful Jesus. Amen.

FEEDING THE
FIVE THOUSAND

John 6:1-14

After these things Jesus went over the Sea of Galilee, which is the Sea of Tiberias. Then a great multitude followed Him, because they saw His signs which He performed on those who were diseased. And Jesus went up on the mountain, and there He sat with His disciples.

Now the Passover, a feast of the Jews, was near. Then Jesus lifted up His eyes, and seeing a great multitude coming toward Him, He said to Philip, "Where shall we buy bread, that these may eat?" But this He said to test him, for He Himself knew what He would do.

Philip answered Him, "Two hundred denarii worth of bread is not sufficient for them, that every one of them may have a little."

One of His disciples, Andrew, Simon Peter's brother, said to Him, "There is a lad here who has five barley loaves and two small fish, but what are they among so many?"

Then Jesus said, "Make the people sit down." Now there was much grass in the place. So the men sat down, in number about five thousand. And Jesus took the loaves, and when He had given thanks He distributed them to the disciples, and the disciples to those sitting down; and likewise of the fish, as much as they wanted. So when they were filled, He said to His disciples, "Gather up the fragments that remain, so that nothing is lost." Therefore they gathered them up, and filled twelve baskets with the fragments of the five barley loaves which were left over by those who had eaten. Then those men, when they had seen the sign that Jesus did, said, "This is truly the Prophet who is to come into the world."

IN THE SIXTH CHAPTER OF JOHN, JESUS FEEDS THE FIVE thousand. And we have to keep in mind that when they talk about five thousand, they're talking about five thousand men. So if the women and the children are figured in, you might have twelve thousand or fifteen thousand people. So it was a huge crowd.

Now, John talks about one miracle in one chapter, and for the next miracle, he starts another chapter. We have to remember that John is not putting in all the events that happened between these miracles. Jesus just didn't move from the pool of Bethesda up onto the heights overlooking the Sea of Galilee, probably the Golan Heights as we know them today. These things didn't take place just one right after another.

When you study and read the Scriptures, you'll notice that there in chapter six, when he comes to the feeding of the five thousand, John says, "After these things..." What things?

Well, if you want to find out all the things that Jesus did between the healing of the paralytic in John 5 and the feeding of the five thousand in John 6, you can read Matthew chapters 5–7 and chapter 13. You can also read from Mark 3:1 on to 6:30. You can look at Luke chapters 6–9. All these chapters fill in what happened between the lifting up of the lame man or the paralytic and the feeding of five thousand. A lot of things happened in that period of time between those two miracles. During this time, Jesus chose the twelve disciples, and he gave the beautiful Beatitudes as he preached that wonderful sermon, the Sermon on the Mount.

Many, many years ago, I had a man tell me, "When you can preach a sermon like the Sermon on the Mount, I'll come to your church." Well of course I couldn't match anything like that, and he never came to the church. So that was one excuse I've heard. I could write a whole book on some of the excuses I've heard from people not wanting to attend church.

Jesus gave the Beatitudes and the Sermon on the Mount. He talked about the house built upon the rock. He gives us the parable of the creditor and the two debtors, and the parable of the sower. Jesus stills the waves. He raises Jairus's daughter, and he heals the woman that had an issue of blood. He sends out the twelve to preach, and he has them come in and give their report. He deals with the maniac of Gadara. All these things happen, and finally you have the beheading of John the Baptist. So there are a lot of things that happen before this sixth chapter of John's Gospel. As a matter of fact, between the time Jesus turned the water into wine at Cana and when he fed the five thousand over the Sea of Galilee, you have a year's time.

So the apostle John is just picking out some miracles, and there's a time lapse between them. And we have to keep that in mind. Jesus has been teaching and traveling and doing these things, which brings us to John 6. As he travels along, the people are getting ready for the Passover, and they're coming from all over to Palestine. They're going to go to Jerusalem.

As they travel along, they're hearing about Jesus doing his miracles, and little by little there are contingencies of people joined together until you have a mob of people— maybe fifteen thousand people coming to listen to Jesus teach and do his miracles.

In many ways, the Passover feast was to the Jews like the Fourth of July is to Americans. It signified their release from Egypt and the formation of their nation. It was a rallying point for intense nationalistic zeal. It was a first class celebration, and everybody and his dog came to it. And as they're traveling to Jerusalem and they're hearing about the teaching, a huge group of people come to follow Jesus.

We're told that this took place on a great plateau east of the Sea of Galilee. That's a beautiful area. I've been there, and it does have grass, especially at Passover time. The people could sit there on the grass. And from the Golan Heights, you can look eastward and you can see the city of Damascus, that ancient city. They claim that it's the oldest continually inhabited city in the world. The setting in John 6 was on this plateau, and when Jesus went forth, he saw a great multitude and was moved with compassion toward them. And he healed their sick.

He was moved with compassion. That's Jesus. Don't ever forget it. That's Jesus. I think the *Living Bible* says, "He pitied them." He saw them in their need. He saw them, and they had such a spiritual need.

Compassion means to suffer with one another. It means to get alongside of somebody and support them, to help and encourage them. Jesus looked at them that way. That's a picture of Jesus. His eye is always upon the multitudes, and especially upon his people. His eye never closes, he never sleeps, and we need to remember that.

He promised that he would never leave us or forsake us. When we are weary, and when we're distressed, and when we're hurt and afraid, and feel all alone, just remember that Jesus knows, and he cares. And his heart aches for you. Every heartbeat you have and every heartache you have, Jesus knows all about it. He's touched with the feelings of our infirmities. He knows and loves and cares. And there's nothing that can dim this truth. He gives the very best to those who leave the choice with him.

So it's been a long day. It's been a hot day. The people followed Jesus out there in the sunlight, listening in the sunshine. As that day comes toward an end, Jesus talks to Philip and he says, "Where shall we buy bread that these may eat?" Now, John is very careful to point out very quickly, "This he said to prove him, for he himself knew what he would do." In other words, he puts a question to Philip. And by the way, this is the only place in the Bible that Jesus ever asked anybody for advice. He did ask various questions to people, but as far as asking for advice, he never asked it except here to Philip. But it's not that Jesus didn't know what to do. He knew already. John says, "He knew what he was going to do, but he did it to test Philip." He wanted Philip to put his faith in Jesus. He wanted Philip to grow. He wanted him to become strong. He wanted him to think. So he asked him that question, and Philip answered, "Oh, two hundred pennyworth of bread is not sufficient for them."

In other words, as the *New International Version* says here, Philip answered him, "Eight months' wages would not buy enough food for each one to have a bite." When I hear that, I think of those little sandwiches they have about as big as a dollar coin. You could take six of those sandwiches and eat them in one gulp and have half a meal.

So Philip says, "If we had a man work almost a year and he gave us all his wages to buy food for this multitude, then each person here would get just a snack." They'd get one of those little sandwiches. And what good is that? It's more of an aggravation than anything.

Then comes Andrew, and he says, "I found somebody here, I found a lad, and he has five barley loaves and two small fish." Then Andrew thinks, "What am I talking about? I must be crazy." So he says, "But what are they among so many?" It's like saying, "What a stupid thing! I bring in this little boy with these five barley loaves and the two little smelly fish, and here we have maybe fifteen thousand people, and what are they amongst so many?" Andrew thinks, "Am I crazy to mention this sort of thing?" He kind of retracts it.

Five barley loaves. Barley was the coarsest of bread. The poorest of the poor ate barley loaves. And those little fish probably were pickled fish from the Sea of Galilee. They had a luxury of fresh fish all over. So the whole Roman Empire knew about these little pickled fish that were caught from the Sea of Galilee. Sounds appetizing, doesn't it?

But Andrew brings over the little lad. And you have to just remember the wonder of this little boy. He gives his lunch. Now, you talk about a sacrifice. You ever see a little boy that wasn't hungry? They're all hungry, all the time. And he has a lunch, and it's toward the end of day. His mother has packed it for him. She said, "Don't you eat this until you get toward the end of the day, so you have some strength."

But the little boy gave the whole thing to Jesus, and that's when things started to happen. Jesus said, "Make them sit down." In other words, Jesus is a God of order. He says, "Sit down." We're not told that in John's account, but we're told this by one of the other apostles. And Jesus says, "Sit down in fifties and hundreds." He's a God of order and decency. And whether we play or we work or we worship, God says that he wants it to be done decently and in order. Even when they came out of Egypt, he had them in groups of five put together. There's always to be order in God's business.

Then Jesus took the loaves and fish, and he gave thanks. And that's something that Jesus is teaching us today. Don't take a bite of food without giving thanks. Sometimes we think, "Well, what if it's just a cookie? Should we give thanks?" Well, I guess if it doesn't have calories, or if it's a Diet Coke, maybe the best thing to do is go ahead and drink it without giving thanks. Because you can drink all the Diet Coke you want, and I'd never give thanks for it. I don't like it one bit. But the genuine thing— you give thanks for that.

If you're at home or in a restaurant, give thanks. That's a witness. Jesus gave thanks, and he let everybody know that every morsel of food we have comes from the Father in heaven.

It's been said that if the sun was blotted out of the sky so that nothing could grow, the whole world would starve within six weeks' time. That's how close we are to starving. But this God supplies, and he gives us these things.

So they gave thanks. And when they were all done, Jesus said, "Don't waste a thing. Put the leftover food in the refrigerator." Jesus is saying, "You're going to save it. Don't you waste anything." And they got twelve baskets full of leftovers. You may ask, "Why did he have just twelve?" I think he had twelve because he had twelve disciples, and they were worrying how they were going to feed the multitude. But the next day, they were carrying a great, big old, heavy basket over their back. And they were sweating it out, and struggling along, and remembering, "Look what Jesus can do." He taught them a lesson.

Now he's teaching us something spiritual here. I see four things.

I see, first of all, that this wonderful story is telling us there's absolutely no problem that Jesus can't handle. There is no problem but what Jesus can handle it. Philip was worrying, Andrew was worrying, but they forgot to work Jesus into their equation.

I hear about people who'd like to do this and they'd like to do that for God. They would like to do so many things. But if we leave Jesus out, we have problems. In your daily living, you have to just remember that we have a great God, and he has all power.

Jeremiah said, "Ah, Lord God, behold, thou hast made the heavens and the earth by thy great power, and by thine outstretched arm; nothing is too difficult for thee." Nothing is too difficult for Jesus. And God answers, and he affirms what Jeremiah says. God says, "Behold." This is in Jeremiah 32: "Behold, I am the Lord, the God of all flesh. Is there anything too difficult for me?" That's in the Old Testament. And in the New Testament, Luke says, "For nothing will be impossible with God." He says again, "The things impossible with men are possible with God."

Don't underestimate the power of Jesus Christ. He can handle any problem in your life, in my life, in the church's life, in our country's life, and in the world's life. He can handle it all.

I remember Charles Swindoll saying about this miracle that when Philip and Andrew saw the impossible circumstances surrounding them, Philip looked first at the budget, and Andrew checked the pantry, but neither of them thought to look to the Lord.

Seems strange, doesn't it? Particularly after they'd seen him change water into wine, but then don't we respond in much the same way?

We've all seen Jesus work miracles in our lives. We've seen him change the old water of our lives into new wine. We've seen him give new legs of faith to our lame spiritual bodies. And yet when faced with impossible circumstances, how soon we forget the power of our God. He says, "The next time you're faced with the impossible, try not to look at your bank account or into your cupboards. Look first to Jesus, the bread of life who can do exceeding, abundantly above all that we ask or think."

So the next time you have trouble, the next time you're out of a job, the next time the kids don't go right, the next time you have some sickness, or the next time your health fails, look to Jesus. Figure that into the equation. He can do all things.

There's something else this tells me—that there's no person too small for God to use. Andrew comes, and he has this little boy with the loaves and the fish, but what are they among so many? But we need to remember that with God, there isn't anything that's too small. God can use the smallest and the tiniest. He can use the little children. There's nothing too small for God to use. But you say, I don't have any money. I don't have any education. I can't speak. I can't sing. I can't do anything. But you give yourself to Christ and his kingdom, and God will use you. But you've got to give yourself to him. Hold on to him without reservation.

Look at the Bible. God used a tiny baby's tear to touch the heart of Pharaoh's daughter, and it changed the whole course of history. He used the shepherd rod of Moses to perform mighty miracles in Egypt. He used the sling of young David to bring down the gigantic Philistine giant. He used a little maid to bring mighty Naaman to Elisha for healing. And he used the widow with a handful of flour to sustain his prophet Elijah. He used a little child to teach his great disciples the lesson of humility. He used the widow's example of sacrificial giving, though tiny in amount, to challenge the whole world for giving.

He took a little boy here with the lunch, and he used it for his honor and glory. God does that. He uses the little things that are given to God. Somebody has said, "You may be too big for God to use you, but you'll never be too little or too small." Every person is important. Even shut-ins and those on beds of sickness can be used of God to be a witness, and to pray, and to shine for Jesus. No matter who we are, God will use us.

William Booth, the founder of the Salvation Army, lived a great life and served God and fed multitudes. Those who knew him said the secret of his ministry and this vast outreach was this: "It was because eighty years ago, God got everything of William Booth." And today the Salvation Army is doing that. So give yourself to God.

Next, I've noticed in this story that Jesus is trying to tell us there's just no future in loaves and fish. There's no future in that. Here they are, five thousand or fifteen thousand people—we don't know exactly how many, and it doesn't matter. They are fed, and they are full, and they are satisfied, and they have food left over. But the next morning they're hungry again. There's got to be more to their life than just loaves and fish. Jesus says, "Man shall not live by bread alone." He's telling us there's a spiritual dimension. Read John 6, because the people never got the lesson, the spiritual lesson. Their hearts were hardened.

Jesus is telling us there's more to life than this bread from heaven. He tries to teach a spiritual lesson. He's telling them that until your soul finds God, until you have that relationship with Jesus Christ, you are never going to be satisfied. We're all made to have communion with God. He made us that way from the beginning. And in the garden of Eden, when Adam and Eve sinned, they broke that relationship.

There's that part of the human psyche or being that says, "We have to have more than the barley loaves and the fish." We have to have the Spirit of God to join our spirits with him, or we'll never find peace and satisfaction and contentment in this world. That's what Jesus is saying.

He could be a living smorgasbord and feed people in a miraculous way every day, day after day after day—and then they die and go to hell. So what's the future of that? Jesus is saying, "You have to come to me. I am the bread of life. And if you'll just eat of me and partake of me, you will have eternal life." Jesus said unto them, "I am the bread of life. He that cometh to me shall never hunger. He that believeth on me shall never thirst." Jesus is moving away now from the physical material bread, the loaves and the fish, and he's saying, "You have to eat of me. You have to take of me. You have to receive me. You have to take me not just in your head but in your heart." And then you're going to find satisfaction.

You'll still need the loaves and the fish, of course, but you'll have that thing that really prompts them. The spirit of the soul will be fed, and will learn to lean on Jesus. Now listen to what Jesus said: "Labor not for the meat that perisheth, but for that meat which endureth to everlasting life, which the Son of man shall give unto you. For him hath God the Father sealed." The people said to him, "What shall we do that we might work the works of God?" And Jesus said unto them, "This is the work of God." You want to know what the work of God is? Jesus tells us. "This is the work of God. Here it is. That you'd believe on him whom he hath sent." That's what it's all about. It's not the barley loaves and the fish and the twelve baskets full. It's the Son of God in your heart and soul.

When we have Jesus, we don't need anything else. It isn't Jesus plus this or that or the other thing. It's just Jesus. It's not Jesus and church membership, or Jesus and some denomination, or Jesus and some creed, or Jesus and baptism, or Jesus and some moral code. It's just Jesus. That's all. And let the others have their part.

John says, "They were all filled." That is, on a physical level, they were filled. And when they take the bread of life, the bread of heaven, they will be filled spiritually.

As much as we want, we'll get more and more of Jesus. As we live out our life and walk with him, we feed on that bread and we're always satisfied. All we need is in Jesus, in this wonderful, wonderful Jesus. Don't you see that?

Paul tells us, "Though our outward man perish"—that's your bread, that's your loaves and your fish. "Though our outward man perish, the inward man is renewed day by day." And when this body decays and when this body gets old and goes to pieces, it's going. That's the way you'll all go. But the inward man gets stronger.

That's where the power is. In the Spirit of God. Why did Jesus feed the five thousand that day? Well, he did it to minister to their immediate needs. He had compassion on them. He felt sorry for them. But far more than that, he was giving a miracle so he could talk about the bread from heaven that will give them eternal life, and they will never hunger nor thirst anymore. Like Jesus says in John 10, "I am come that they might have life." Not physical life, but spiritual life. "I am come that they might have life, and have it more abundantly."

Jesus. The only way is Jesus. He says, "Labor not for the meat which perisheth, but for the meat that endureth unto everlasting life." All we need spiritually is in Jesus. And that's why we feed on Jesus. And that's why, when we come to church on Sunday mornings, we don't come for a circus. We don't come to see what man can do or perform, or any of those things. We come to hear the Word of God, to feed on Jesus. If that isn't enough, then you're feeding on the wrong things.

That's what draws us together. That's what gives us strength. And that's the way we can find Jesus. So we read our Bible, we pray, we go to church, and we never get enough of Jesus. And when we come to church, we come not to see what's wrong with the church, but we come to worship Jesus and to learn of him.

Hungry people are humble people. They're not there to criticize. They're there to feast on Jesus, and they want to be fed.

How hungry are you? Have you taken Jesus as your Savior? Have you taken this wonderful bread of life and fed on him? The people that day on the Golan Heights never caught the message. They became hard, and then they turned against him. Over and over, Jesus was trying to get them to think in the realm of the spiritual. But it's so hard to move from this worldly thing that we can touch and handle, and give it up to that which touches our soul, the soul of the spirit and the heart. You've got to make that transition, and you can make it if you come to Jesus and love Jesus.

"Blessed are they which do hunger and thirst after righteousness," Jesus said, "for they shall be filled." I hope and I pray your trust in Jesus.

Dear heavenly Father, thank you for the bread of life. We can take that wonderful bread of life, and we will never die. We'll leave this body and leave this earth, but we'll never die. We'll be with you forever. May there be multitudes today who will put their faith in your Son Jesus, asking him to come into their heart and life, to save them from their sin, and who will then begin to follow you. We pray this in Jesus's name. Amen.

OPENING
BLIND EYES

John 9:1-12

Now as Jesus passed by, He saw a man who was blind from birth. And His disciples asked Him, saying, "Rabbi, who sinned, this man or his parents, that he was born blind?"

Jesus answered, "Neither this man nor his parents sinned, but that the works of God should be revealed in him. I must work the works of Him who sent Me while it is day; the night is coming when no one can work. As long as I am in the world, I am the light of the world."

When He had said these things, He spat on the ground and made clay with the saliva; and He anointed the eyes of the blind man with the clay. And He said to him, "Go, wash in the pool of Siloam" (which is translated, Sent). So he went and washed, and came back seeing.

Therefore the neighbors and those who previously had seen that he was blind said, "Is not this he who sat and begged?"

Some said, "This is he." Others said, "He is like him."

He said, "I am he."

Therefore they said to him, "How were your eyes opened?"

He answered and said, "A Man called Jesus made clay and anointed my eyes and said to me, 'Go to the pool of Siloam and wash.' So I went and washed, and I received sight."

Then they said to him, "Where is He?"

He said, "I do not know."

Let's look at another miracle that Jesus performed so we can better know him and serve him—the miracle where Jesus opens the eyes of a blind man. It starts in the ninth chapter of John with the words, "And as Jesus passed by, he saw a man who was blind from his birth."

Although we don't know where Jesus had been, and we don't know the interval of time, most Bible teachers feel that Jesus had just had his time of confrontation with the Pharisees in the temple. Following that, he began to walk the streets of Jerusalem. And he comes to a place near the pool of Siloam, and he sees a man who is blind. It really doesn't matter the order of events so much, but we try to place them if we possibly can.

So the disciples see a man blind from birth, and they ask Jesus a question. They say, "Master, who sinned—this man, or his parents—that he was born blind?"

Now they ask that because the people of that day had the philosophy that if somebody's sick, then somebody has to have sinned. And if anybody is sick, then you are a sinner. Please note, we're all sinners, but they feel like there's some special sin that makes you sick. Of course, people that think that way are sick, because there isn't any truth to that at all. As we look in Scripture, we find that there are people who have that as their philosophy. If somebody's sick, then they've sinned.

Of course, when you think about Job and his friends, that was their philosophy. They came to Job and they said, "Look here, Job. You've had all these calamities, and why don't you confess your sin so God can forgive you and heal you?" Job insists that he hasn't done anything wrong that he knows of. He's served the Lord the best he can, and he's righteous with God.

Job was right, because God out of heaven called Job the most righteous man of his day. So Job isn't somebody who just thinks that he's a righteous man, but God out of heaven says he's the most righteous man of his day. And you know the story of Job. His buddies come to him, and the only nice thing you can say about them is that they were quiet for a long time before they spoke. They stayed a day or two while they didn't say anything, and then they start talking. That quiet part was nice.

So the fact of the matter is that Job had not sinned. There was a battle or a debate between God and Satan, and that resulted in Job being tested, and so Job didn't have a thing to do with it, but they were laying this at his door.

That's just exactly what these disciples in John 9 are saying. Here's this man born blind—so who sinned? Did this man sin, or did his parents sin? Now right off the bat you'd say, "If this man was born blind, how could he sin before he was born?" That's a little ridiculous, unless you believe in reincarnation, and you believe in people coming back again and again and again in another life, from one life to another, and if they've been bad in one life they come back in the next life and be under some infirmity. So perhaps some of the disciples were thinking along that line. The Gnostics of that day believed in this preexistent pre-incarnation. They believed that a single soul would come back to earthly life in another form and another form, again and again. So that was a teaching of that day.

You get that from the disciples, when you remember that in Matthew 16, Jesus asked the disciples, "Whom do men say that I the Son of Man am?" They answered, "Some say that thou art John the Baptist, some Elijah; and others, Jeremiah, or one of the prophets." Here they are, they're saying that some think Elijah has come back recycled, or Jeremiah or Elisha or one of the prophets, so they have that mindset. When they ask, "Has this man sinned or somebody else?" they're wondering if this blind man has lived before and is coming back and being punished.

There was even a teaching by some of the rabbis that it was dependent on how the baby was in the womb. If the baby was still and nice, that's fine. But if the baby had caused a lot of commotion, he might be born with some calamity or some infirmity, because he didn't behave in the womb. They liked to talk about the struggle between Jacob and Esau while in Rebecca's womb, and so that was being passed around too.

So when they ask this question, "Did this man sin even before he was born?" they meant it. They asked, "Did this man sin? Or did his parents sin?" Well, that second part was quite possible. We see that every day, don't we? We see these parents who are on drugs, they're drug addicts, and they have babies born with withdrawals. Or we see the heavy smokers and the drinkers bringing little babies into the world with all sorts of problems.

When you think about these things happening—people sitting with a high hand and little babies suffering the sins of the father visited on the children—then the question the disciples asked wasn't such a bad question. So Jesus answers and listen to what Jesus tells them, "First of all, neither has this man sinned nor his parents." He's telling the disciples, "You are wrong on both accounts. The man hasn't sinned and the parents haven't sinned, and this blindness is not a result of his sin or his parent's sin." Well that was something for them to choke on. They never dreamed of such a thing.

Next, notice what Jesus does *not* tell them. Jesus doesn't tell them why the man was born blind. He never told them. He just said, "It isn't the child, and it isn't the parents." You're wrong in your philosophy, and you're wrong with laying this at their door. He says that this isn't this case, but he didn't tell them really why the man was born blind. Keep that in mind. We'll get to that in just a minute.

But first of all, there's a passage of Scripture that some people use. They say that the reason this man was born blind was so that Jesus could show his glory. If you see verses three and four, you'll see Jesus answered, "Neither hath this man sinned, nor his parents: but that the works of God should be made manifest in him. I must work the works of him that sent me, while it is day: the night cometh, when no man can work." Now, if you let those verses stand with that kind of punctuation—and remember that there wasn't any punctuation in these Scriptures as they're written; the punctuation is all man made. But if you let that passage stand the way it is, then you are saying that God brought this little baby in the world blind, and he let him sit there as a beggar and blind for years and years and years for one reason, so Jesus could come and heal him and bring glory to God. If you believe that, then you're saying that God created a man blind so later he could show his power. Now I don't have that kind of a God.

G. Campbell Morgan—a great scholar and a great preacher of London in another age—talks about this. In his commentary on John's Gospel, he changes the punctuation for this passage. He has talked to Greek scholars, and they have said it's very possible it could be punctuated so that it reads, "Neither did this man sin nor his parents"—period. He has answered the disciples. He's set that at rest, put that to bed. Then comes this: "That the works of God should be made manifest in him, I must work the works of him that sent me while it is day." What Jesus is saying is, "Here's a man born blind. He didn't sin, and his parents didn't sin. I'm not going to tell you why he's blind. He's blind, but I'm going to heal him to the glory of God." God doesn't make blind people and let them live in misery all those years just so that he can come and work some miracle in them, like you do rats in some kind of a laboratory.

There is what we call the mystery of iniquity. There is sin in the world, and there's insidious sin in the world that we don't understand and know, and God alone knows. He's telling these men, "This man hasn't sinned, his parents haven't sinned. I'm not going to tell you why he's blind, but I'm going to heal him, to the glory of God."

I've been in the ministry now for over half a century, and over that span of time, I've heard people ask, "Why am I sick? Why do I have cancer? Why did I have this stroke? Why was I born crippled? Why was my loved one taken at a young age? Why did my baby die?" And on and on.

Jesus—dear friend Jesus, wonderful, wonderful Jesus—is telling his disciples, "I cannot explain these things to you now until we get over yonder, so don't you ask, don't speculate, don't guess, don't get angry. Because you're never going to know why in this world."

Sometimes I hear these people who are trying to explain all these things, but you can't explain them. The little baby dies, and the pastor or somebody will say, "Well, God wanted him in heaven more than he wanted him on earth." Well then, why did he give him in the first place, if that's the case? There's a mystery here that we don't know, and God isn't going to tell us. What Jesus says is like what Moses already declared in the Old Testament: "The secret things belong unto the Lord our God." And he's telling them, "I'm not going to tell you why. I'm just not going to give you the answer." So just say, "Dear God, I don't understand."

I have these questions just like you do. A wonderful Christian brother of mine, a pastor, died in a plane crash leaving five little children, and there isn't any explanation. So what are we to do?

We say, "Dear God, what do you want me to do? This trial has come into my life, this sorrow has come into my life, and I'm going to lean upon you, and I'm going to trust you. I'm going to place things into your hands." That's what Paul did. He had a thorn in the flesh, he didn't know why, but he said, "I'm going to grow for God in this infirmity, and I'm going to bring glory to his name through my suffering and sorrow."

That's what Job did. He lost everything, his every possession, except for his wife. I don't know if she's a possession or not, but his wife said to Job, "Why don't you curse God and die?" And what did Job say? "I don't understand these things. I wish I could know. But I don't care if he slays me also—I'm trusting my God."

That's what Jesus is telling those disciples. This man didn't sin, his parents didn't sin, and I'm not going to tell you why that man was born blind. But you trust me and you love me, and you leave that up to me.

William Barclay in his *Daily Study Bible* has a great statement: "Disappointment, loss, always are opportunities for displaying God's grace." And he says, "It enables the suffering to show God in action."

When trouble and disaster fall upon a man who doesn't know God, that man may well collapse, but when they fall on a man who walks with God, they bring out the strength and the beauty and the endurance and the nobility which are within a man's heart, when God is there in his heart.

It is told that when an old saint was dying in agony of pain, he sent for his family and said, "Come and see how a Christian can die." It's when life hits us a terrible blow that we can show the world how a Christian can live, and if need be, how to die. Any kind of suffering is an opportunity to demonstrate the glory of God in our lives, and that's what we need to do. We need to trust and believe in the sovereignty of a loving God, and submit to him, and shine and bring glory to his name.

Let's look at the problem in John 9. The problem is that there's a man who was blind from his birth. A blind man, that's nothing new to see in the Middle East. You'll see them all over the place. Begging is about all they can do. Sometimes they have a little musical instrument, a violin or something, and they'll play, and they'll have a place where you can leave some money for them. I saw one place where a little baby was lying on a newspaper right out in the bright sun, and the mother was sitting there by that baby to see if they could get some money. There are many blind people. Bishop Ryle has noted that the Gospels record more cases of blindness healed than any other affliction. There was one deaf and dumb person who was healed, and one sick with palsy, and one sick with fever. There are two instances of lepers being healed, and three dead persons raised to life. Meanwhile there are five blind persons who were healed. And so this blindness was prevalent.

You know what this blindness tells us? It speaks about people who don't know Jesus Christ. It's an illustration of people who don't know Christ, the light of the world.

Spiritually they're blinded, and they don't understand the things of God. They don't understand his ways, and they don't trust God, because they're in blackness and darkness. It's an illustration of a person who doesn't know Jesus Christ personally.

It all came about with Adam and Eve. Something awful happened with our first parents in the garden of Eden that made us all blind, blind as a bat spiritually. That blindness passed on to all human beings. Adam was placed in the garden of Eden, and you know the story. He had a perfect environment, and everything was his, and his body was the temple of God. But one day he disobeyed God. Remember what God had told him? He said, "Adam, you can eat anything in the garden, anything your heart desires. Eat it until you bust if you want to, you can eat anything you want. But I've got one tree over there, and that one is out of bounds. If you eat of that tree, you're going to die."

Listen to God: "The Lord God commanded the man, saying, Of every tree of the garden thou mayest freely eat: but of the tree of the knowledge of good and evil, thou shalt not eat of it: for in the day that thou eatest thereof thou shall surely die."

So guess what? Adam couldn't get his eyes off that tree. He fell in love with the tree. And before he knew it, like a moth drawn to a flame, he was there and he ate of the tree. And guess what? Before you can say apple, he was dead spiritually. The light left him and he was in darkness and blackness.

The whole human race was represented in Adam. We fell with him, and we're in that same darkness and that same blackness. Spiritually, we're all dead as a mackerel and blind as a bat—the whole world.

So God tells us something very enlightening in John's Gospel, in the first chapter and the fourth verse. He says, "In him [that is, in Jesus] was life, and the life was the light of men." Jesus is the life, and that life is the light of man. But when Adam sinned, the life was gone, and when the life was gone, the lights went out, and he was in blindness. He lost that light of life that he had known. He didn't die physically right away, though he did die some years later, but he died spiritually the moment he ate of that forbidden fruit. I don't know if that fruit was an apple or a persimmon or whatever; the Bible doesn't say, and it doesn't matter. The Bible is talking about disobeying God. And Adam became blind.

And in John 9, when we see this blind man begging on the streets of Jerusalem, he's in total darkness, just as Adam was in total darkness, and the whole world was in total darkness. Listen to what Jesus tells us in Matthew's Gospel: "The people that sat in darkness saw a great light, and to them that sat in the region and shadow of death, life is sprung up." The whole world fell with Adam, and the whole world was in darkness. The Scriptures tell us in 1 Corinthians 15, "For as in Adam all die, even so in Christ shall all be made alive." And Jesus tells Nicodemus, "Unless you're born again, you can never see the kingdom of God, because you're blind."

You've got to have Christ, and you've got to have that experience of asking Jesus Christ personally to come into life and save you, for Christ's sake. It doesn't matter how old you are. It doesn't matter how cultured you are. It doesn't matter how many degrees you have. It doesn't matter how rich you are. You are blind spiritually if you don't have Christ. Satan tries to keep people in blindness, in the darkness, in the kingdom of darkness. He doesn't want you to believe, and he doesn't want you to accept Jesus Christ. When you put this decision off, you're just falling into Satan's hands. The Scriptures tell us, "If our gospel be hid, it is hid to them that are lost, in whom the God of this world [Satan] has blinded the minds of them which believe not, lest the light of the glorious gospel of Christ, who is the image of God, should shine unto them."

That's the problem. But we have the solution—Jesus himself. Jesus is the way out. There is only one way out, but there is that way out, and when people come out of this darkened world and are transferred from the kingdom of darkness into the kingdom of light, that's receiving Christ. You can have that spiritual eyesight, and you can have that eternal life that God will give you through faith in his Son.

I'm going to tell you, friend: The most terrible and wicked sin you can commit is to reject Jesus Christ. It's the most terrible sin you can commit, and there is no help out of it. When the judgment is given for the people who are blind and who refuse Jesus Christ, there is only condemnation and judgment—awful, awful judgment.

The light of Christ can be close to you, but you've got to let it shine, and you've got to ask it in. My dear friend, you can go to church, you can even enjoy church, you can enjoy the scene—the music and the singing and all the rest of it. You might even enjoy the sermon or parts of it. You might sing in the choir, or shake people's hands. But unless you have that personal acceptance of Jesus Christ, you're a poor lost sinner. You need to admit and confess that you're a poor lost sinner, and that you're blind and you're poor and you're naked. Your works are like filthy rags, and you're alone and you're destitute, and there's no place to turn and no place to hide. You need to confess that you're a blind beggar and call upon Christ Jesus to save you.

Jesus said, "Night cometh when no man can work." If you're in the darkness, there's going to come a greater darkness that's going to settle on you forever and ever in hell. But there's the wonderful light of the world, if you come to Jesus. Work must be done and decisions must be made while it is day, before the night comes down.

Maybe you've had opportunities to accept Christ, but you've turned him down. You ought to pray and ask Christ to come into your heart and save you. You ought to go on record as being a follower of Jesus Christ.

This blind man that we meet in John 9 becomes saved. He gets the light, and he gives us a challenge. The challenge is that when he found the light and he was able to see, that wasn't the end of the story, but the beginning of the story. When he was given his sight and he was healed by Jesus, he doesn't even know who Jesus is. He's never seen Jesus. He's been blind from birth. He didn't know Jesus of Nazareth from anybody else. He didn't know a thing about Jesus, but he was given his sight.

Now the Pharisees are there in the crowd. They're all upset because Jesus did this on the Sabbath. I think he did it purposely on the Sabbath to teach them a lesson, but the Pharisees hated him for it, and they never forgave him, and they finally put him on the cross. So they come to this man who'd been blind and they say, "How were your eyes opened?" He doesn't know how his eyes were opened. He just says (in John 9:11), "A man who is called Jesus made clay, and I received my sight." But the Pharisees won't give up on it, so they keep badgering him and pushing him. Pretty soon he says, "Well, he was a prophet." He's starting to think, and he says, "Hey, this takes more than just a man. This can't be a sinner like the Pharisees are saying, so he's got to be a prophet."

He tells them, "A prophet came." And the Pharisees won't give up; they push and they push and they push. Soon, for this man, the light is dawning, and he's growing in his faith. He says, "A man sent from God. God healed me."

Now the point I want you to see is that when we accept Jesus Christ, we have to grow in that faith. We have to do everything we can to grow. Read the Bible and pray and talk with Christian friends and go to Christian places. Be careful what you watch on television, and be in church if you possibly can, and be listening to the Word of God.

Paul talks about this in Romans 1:17, where he says, "For therein is the righteousness of God revealed from faith to faith: as it is written, the just shall live by faith." It's from faith to faith. It happened to this man. With just a little faith, he calls Jesus a man. With a little more faith, he says, "He is a prophet." With a little more faith he says, "He's a prophet sent from God." With a little more faith he says, "He's God Almighty." And that's what God wants us to do. In the Proverbs we read, "The path of the just is as the shining light, that shineth more and more unto the perfect day."

So, dear friend, we just have to come to Jesus Christ, admitting that we're blind and we're poor and we're a beggar, and we don't have a thing, and we ask him to save us. Just call on his name.

Jesus says, "Him that cometh to me I will in no wise cast out." Once you've found him, then serve him, walk with him, glorify his name. Don't try to answer all the questions; just love him. Trust in the sovereignty of God, because he's a God who gave his Son for you. You can trust that kind of sovereignty. You can trust the wonderful, wonderful Jesus.

Thank you, heavenly Father, for your dear Son Jesus. Thank you for telling us that as many as received him, to them he gave power to become children of God, even to those who believe on his name. May there be many today who will make that prayer, and be taken out of that kingdom of darkness, and become a part of the kingdom of light. And then help them to grow, grow, grow. In Jesus's name, Amen.

THE RAISING
OF LAZARUS

John 11:38-44

Then Jesus, again groaning in Himself, came to the tomb. It was a cave, and a stone lay against it. Jesus said, "Take away the stone."

Martha, the sister of him who was dead, said to Him, "Lord, by this time there is a stench, for he has been dead four days."

Jesus said to her, "Did I not say to you that if you would believe you would see the glory of God?" Then they took away the stone from the place where the dead man was lying. And Jesus lifted up His eyes and said, "Father, I thank You that You have heard Me. And I know that You always hear Me, but because of the people who are standing by I said this, that they may believe that You sent Me." Now when He had said these things, He cried with a loud voice, "Lazarus, come forth!" And he who had died came out bound hand and foot with graveclothes, and his face was wrapped with a cloth. Jesus said to them, "Loose him, and let him go."

IF YOU'RE LIKE I AM, YOU'VE ALWAYS BEEN INTRIGUED with this story of the raising of Lazarus. I remember studying that when we went to a little one-room schoolhouse out in western South Dakota, and in Sunday school we heard the story of Lazarus. The name Lazarus means "God is my help." His name is also translated in other places as Eleazar.

Lazarus fell sick, and he was nigh unto death. He was about to die. For too many people, the last thing they want to happen is to die. Then there are others who just can't wait for death. Christians are rejoicing as we think about going to be with the Lord, but there are other people who don't know the Lord, and they are disgusted with life and what it has to hold. They're not happy, and they're not completely enjoying life.

For instance, Benjamin Disraeli was a nineteenth-century British leader. He talked about life in this way: "Life is a blunder, manhood a struggle and old age a regret."

Shakespeare's character Macbeth says that life is "a tale told by an idiot, full of sound and fury signifying nothing."

The writer George Santayana said, "Life is not a spectacle or a feast. It is a predicament."

Samuel Butler said, "Life is one long process of getting tired."

The French say, "Life is an onion; one cries while peeling it."

These are from ages past, but college students today also define life in not too glowing terms. When asked to give a definition of life, one of these young people said, "Life is a joke that isn't even funny." Another defined life as "a disease for which the only cure is death." Another said, "Life is a jail sentence that we get for the crime of being born." And so on and on. They're not too happy with life.

Dr. Jack Kevorkian was known as Doctor Death for promoting assisted suicide. In the TV movie *You Don't Know Jack,* based on Kevorkian's life, he is asked, "Have you no religion? Have you no God?" And the Kevorkian character answers, "Oh, I do, lady, I have a religion, his name is Bach. Johann Sebastian Bach. And at least my God isn't an invented one."[10]

All kinds of things are said about life and about death.

Jesus said, "I have come to give them life [to give *you* life!] and to give it more abundantly." And Jesus says, "I am coming." Maybe you fear death, and maybe you're bored with death, and maybe you're tired of living, and maybe you're sick and tired of the same old routine. Jesus said, "I'm going to come. I came to give you what I call is really life, full and abundant. A life you can enjoy. A life that has purpose and meaning, and a life that has a beautiful ending with God in heaven."

Now, Satan comes along, and the Scriptures tell us that he comes to do just the opposite. He comes to kill and destroy and to steal. All too many times, he succeeds, so that with many people, life is very, very difficult and hard.

The miracle of raising Lazarus from the dead and giving him life gives us a picture of what life can really be. I want to look at that in this miracle that John records.

First of all, we'll look at how Mary and Martha made a call for help. Then we want to see some lessons to learn in this whole story, and finally, an illustration that I want you to remember.

There was a call for help. Jesus is at a place about twenty miles from Bethany, where Mary and Martha lived. He's there with his disciples, and a distance of about twenty miles would be a day's journey for most people.

One day a messenger comes from Bethany and he gives Jesus this message from Mary and Martha. All the message says is, "Lord, behold, he whom thou loveth is sick." That's all. It's in verse three in the eleventh chapter of John's Gospel: "Lord, behold, he whom thou loveth is sick." The sisters undoubtedly felt that Jesus would come immediately, because they knew that Jesus loved them and he loved Lazarus. They thought he would come immediately.

When you read this story, Jesus doesn't get there until four days after Lazarus dies. The timetable would read like this. The first day it took the messenger all day to get to where Jesus was. On the second day, the messenger returned to Bethany, while Jesus stayed where he was, and then he stayed another day. Only then did Jesus travel all day to Bethany to go to this death scene.

Now, it's very interesting that in their message to Jesus, Mary and Martha didn't tell him what to do. They just said, "He whom thou loveth is sick." I think we better be very careful here because too many times in our prayers we're instructing God and we're telling God.

Sometimes I get the cold chills when I hear these people say, "You have to command God, and then you get things done." When we go to prayer, we have to be like Mary and Martha. They stated their case.

We tell God what's on our heart. We tell him what we would like. We explain it to him and tell him the best we can, and then we close our prayer by saying, "Thy will be done on earth as it is in heaven." That's the way we close our prayers in Jesus's name. There are some things Mary and Martha didn't understand, but they didn't say, "Lazarus is sick, come running." They just said, "Lazarus is sick. You love him. He's sick."

They knew he would come, and they thought he would come quicker than he did. Why did he tarry? Why did he wait? Jesus tells us why he waited, in the fourth verse. He says, "This sickness is not unto death, but for the glory of God, that the Son of God might be glorified thereby." Sometimes we're mystified with the events of life, like Mary and Martha. It baffled them that Jesus didn't come immediately. I can tell you one thing, that it hurt Jesus as much as it hurt these sisters. Jesus loved this family dearly, and he had no home on earth, but he found a home there in Bethany, where Mary and Martha and Lazarus lived.

It hurt Jesus when he saw them hurt. If you are a parent or a grandparent, you know that you would rather be sick yourself than see your little child sick. You'd rather have that sickness than have a grandchild sick. And so Jesus's heart goes out to them. It's not easy for him to wait, but he does wait. Jesus is teaching something here. He's teaching us that he doesn't always act the way we want him to act or expect him to act. He doesn't always shelter us from the storms and problems of life. Lazarus died. As a matter of fact, when you read this story, you find out that when the messenger first got to Jesus, Lazarus was already dead, although the messenger didn't know it. But by the timetable and schedule of these events, he was already dead.

If Jesus doesn't come immediately, it's always for a purpose. That purpose is what we're being shown here, along with Martha and Mary. That is, Jesus wants to strengthen our faith and he wants to glorify God. That's really what we want, isn't it? And so he tarries. He knows: "I'm going to have him die, and he's going to be in the grave four days. I'm going to raise him from the dead, and it's going to be to the glory of God."

Earlier we talked about the man born blind, and there's a similar kind of statement, but it's a totally different story, because with the man born blind, he lived all of his life in darkness and blindness and begging. Jesus was saying, "Here's a blind man and we're not going to spend all our time investigating the whys and the wherefores, but we're going to heal him to the glory of God."

Now with Lazarus, it was a totally different thing. Four days he's in the tomb. It's another story. It's short-term. Jesus let the four days lapse so there could be no question about his power of raising from the dead. I am constantly hearing about these people dying and coming back to life again and selling books about it. I haven't heard yet of anyone who has been dead for four days, and then comes back to life and writes a book about it. When he comes around, I'll buy his book.

This is a miracle here that we just cannot pass by. Jesus talks to his disciples, and he tells them something that's been misinterpreted by a lot of people. Jesus saith unto them, "Our friend Lazarus sleepeth, but I go that I may awake him out of sleep." The disciples are happy because they said, "Well, if he's sleeping, then the fever is gone and the sickness is gone and he's resting." Then said Jesus unto them plainly, "Lazarus is dead." Now we have people going around today and they say, "Well, death is nothing but sleep. You're just put in the grave and you're asleep."

You're just sleeping there until forever and ever, or maybe until God will come. They don't teach that the body is on the earth and the soul is with the Lord. They take a scripture like this in John 11, or they'll take the scripture of when Jesus raised the daughter of Jairus. We read in Matthew 9:24 that Jesus said she was asleep. Or when Stephen was martyred and we read in Acts 7 that at last he fell asleep. Or Paul talks in 1 Corinthians 15:6 of how most of those who were witnesses of the resurrection of Jesus were still alive, though some had fallen asleep.

There's a whole group of people running around saying that after death you're in the grave, the body's in the grave, the person's in the grave. I even heard of one man who one wintry night, went out and put a blanket over his wife's grave so she wouldn't get cold in the night. By going to that extreme, he must have had a guilty conscience about something.

The Bible teaches that after death we are absent from the body and at home with the Lord, and when he talks about sleep he's simply saying the body is put in repose, like it is asleep.

So Jesus gets the message about Lazarus being sick, and he answers, and he comes four days after Lazarus has died.

Now, I want you to see some lessons here. When Jesus and the disciples get to Bethany, Lazarus has been in the grave for four days. The sisters are distraught. Their hearts ache and their hearts are sick. There's a commotion. People are crying and weeping. The Jewish people, like the Arabs, will wail and moan at the grave. I've heard them do that in Lebanon and some of those places. They carry on because they don't have much of a hope beyond the grave.

Jesus goes to Mary and to Martha and he says, "Thy brother shall rise again." Martha doesn't catch it, and she says, "I know that he shall rise again in the resurrection at the last day." In verse 24 of John 11, Martha is missing it, and she's thinking only of that great resurrection when Jesus comes again. He had taught them about that, and they picked that up.

But Jesus is really saying, "I'm going to raise him right now." Jesus promised her one of the most beautiful promises in all of the Bible. I wish I knew how many times I've used this verse in sermons. Jesus said unto her, "I am the resurrection and the life. He that believeth in me, though he were dead, yet shall he live. Whosoever liveth and believeth in me shall never die." *Never die.*

Think of that promise. That's eternal life. When we have that eternal life, we never die. After departing earth, we go into heaven if we have Jesus as our Savior. Adrian Rogers has a little paragraph on that. He says, "It is impossible for those who know the Lord to die. If you're a believer in Jesus Christ, and you want to meet a person who cannot die, take a look in the mirror. You might say, 'Now, wait a minute. We're all going to die.' Wrong. It's absolutely impossible for a bona fide believer in Jesus Christ to die. I didn't say that; Jesus did: 'Whosoever liveth and believeth in me shall never die.'"

Dwight L. Moody is quoted as saying, "Someday you'll read in the papers that D. L. Moody is dead. Don't you believe a word of it! At that moment I shall be more alive than I am now."[11]

Jesus is telling Martha that Lazarus is alive, that he's going to live. He has eternal life and he may be with the Lord. He's going to be called back. He's going to live right now. "Whosoever liveth and believeth in me shall never, ever die."

Adrian Rogers tells a story about a man called Charlie Fisher.

Charlie Fisher was a little wiry guy, whom we used to call Uncle Charlie. I believe he was more on fire for Jesus than any man I've ever known. Uncle Charlie was a member of the church I used to pastor in Fort Pierce, Florida. He had an old canvas-covered airplane that he would use for a very unusual form of witnessing. He would fly over county fairs and drop out bushels of tracts. Then Uncle Charlie would fly back over the place with a loud speaker and preach to the people on the ground, telling them about the Lord Jesus. He would also conduct street meetings and do all kinds of strange things to spread the faith. I could tell you many stories about Uncle Charlie Fisher, but I think the strangest thing Uncle Charlie ever did was to preach his own funeral.

Uncle Charlie told his son, "When I die, just gather my friends around for the funeral. You don't have to do anything. Just gather my friends. I recorded my message. All you have to do is push the play button."

That's exactly what happened. Charlie Fisher preached his own funeral. When the day came, all of Charlie's friends were there. Uncle Charlie's body was there, but he wasn't. Someone pushed the button on the tape recorder and the people heard, "Hello friends. This is Charlie Fisher. I'm up here in heaven and it is wonderful." Then Charlie proceeded to tell all about heaven, how wonderful it was, and then he ended by saying, "I want all of you down there to come and meet me up here in heaven."

I guess that's what it means when the book of Hebrews says of Abel that "he being dead yet speaketh." I've thought of doing the same thing that Charlie Fisher did, to be honest about it. I've thought about maybe having a recording to preach my own funeral. I've thought about that, but then I thought, "Good grief. They'll come to the funeral and say, 'We've heard that guy for a hundred years, and even at his funeral we're going to have to hear him.' They'll grumble, and I don't want anybody grumbling at my funeral. I've had enough of it in my lifetime." So I'm not going to be preaching my own funeral.

Then we read in John 11:35, "Jesus wept." And that tells the sorrow of his heart. That shows us something here, because what is Jesus doing? He's standing there at the tomb, and he's going to raise Lazarus within minutes, and he knows it. Martha doesn't know it, Mary doesn't know it, but Jesus knows it, and yet when he sees them in sorrow, he weeps. Now, if I would have been there, I wouldn't have wept, because I know in a few seconds, a few minutes, Lazarus is going to be raised. You see, I'm not as sensitive as Jesus. Even though he knows it's just minutes until Lazarus is raised, his heart is broken for his people.

Whenever you have a sorrow, whenever you have a problem or a trial—and perhaps today you're going through some deep waters—know that Jesus is weeping with you. You're not weeping alone. He cares and he loves you. Always remember, he is a sympathizing Jesus. Jesus loves you. He cares. He wept, and it shows his heart.

Then Jesus does something, and this is the big illustration that I want you to see.

If you like to read thrillers, here's one at the top of the list, and here's how the account went. Jesus wept, as I've just mentioned, and then Jesus went to the grave. It was a cave with a rock in front of it. Jesus commands that the stone be rolled away, and Martha protests. She says, "You can't do that because by this time, he's been dead four days and there's a stench." She couldn't see any hope for this situation at all.

Then Jesus reminds Martha of the message that he sent her three days before. He said, "This sickness is not unto death, but for the glory of God, that the Son of God might be glorified thereby." When Martha heard that, it strengthened her faith, and she consents to have them roll back the stone.

Then Jesus prays. He thanks God for what he's going to do. He hasn't even done it yet, and he thanks God, because he knows the will of God so perfectly, and he has such strong faith. Sometimes we do that. We thank God for what he's going to do. Jesus thanked God for what's going to come forth.

Then Jesus says, "Lazarus, come forth." He says it "with a loud voice," we read. No incantations, no humble, mumble, bumble stuff, but loud and clear. Let your yes be yes and your no be no. Jesus says, "Lazarus, come forth."

I read where someone said, "Why did he call Lazarus by name?" Well, if he wouldn't have called him by name, the whole Bethany cemetery would have come out of the graves, and they wouldn't have known what to do." So Jesus said, "Lazarus—just you, Lazarus—you come forth."

Then Lazarus comes forth, and Jesus said, "Loose him and let him go."

I want you to see three things in this story.

First of all, I want you to see that Lazarus was dead physically, but not spiritually, and he is a picture of all the world of people who are outside of Christ, who are dead spiritually. They are just as dead as Lazarus was after being in the grave four days. Ephesians 2:1 says, "And you hath he quickened, made alive, who were dead." Dead. Dead as a mackerel in your sins.

You remember what Jesus said? "Let the dead bury the dead." He just simply meant, let the spiritually dead bury the physically dead. That happens every time. I think of this a lot of times when I have funerals. If I have an unsaved undertaker there, unsaved mortician, that's just what's happening. We've got a spiritually dead man burying a physically dead man. That happens sometimes, unfortunately.

The point is simply this. There is no "spark of divinity" in any person. There isn't "a little bit of God" in just any person. There's a place for God to fill, and you're never satisfied and complete until that spiritual part of you is filled by God himself. You don't have any spark of divinity, because any person, if he's dead, is dead. He's not part dead or two-thirds dead. He's dead, or he's alive. This man is dead and so those outside of Jesus Christ are dead.

Jesus spelled it out as plain as day. He said, "He that believeth on the Son hath everlasting life. He that believeth not the Son shall not see life, but the wrath of God abideth on him" (John 3:36). Now, someday when you have a little time and you don't know what to do, try to write it any plainer than that. If you have the Son, you have life. If you don't have the Son, you have death—eternal death, and condemnation, and the judgment and the wrath of God.

The first thing I want you to see is that this man Lazarus is dead physically, and is a picture of a whole world lost in sin. But we have the key. We have the key, who is Jesus Christ, and we better get the word out.

The second thing I notice here is that Jesus has the power to raise Lazarus, who has been dead for four days. And if he can raise Lazarus after four days—if he has the power to raise Lazarus after four days of decomposition—then he's got enough power to handle any problem that you or I might have today.

If Jesus can take care of that dead man, that decomposed body, and bring him back and have him walk out of that tomb, then he can help you and he can help me, no matter what the problem and the difficulty might be. So trust him. Trust him.

Maybe it isn't going to happen in a moment's time. Maybe it's not going to happen the minute that you pray. Sometimes God will say, "No, I'm not going to take you out of the storm. You've got to go through the storm, and then you'll have a bigger victory going through the storm than being delivered from it." Sometimes he'll say, "Wait a little bit. It isn't time yet."

Sometimes he says no, but no is an answer.

God has the power. If it's his will—and that's all we're interested in, his will—then "Thy will be done" no matter what it is. Always, always be in the will of God, because that's where you have peace and contentment and joy and happiness and fulfillment. You don't have it out in the world, carrying on and carousing around like some of the world does. God might not always say yes, but he'll always hear your prayers.

There's one prayer he always says yes to. There's one prayer you can pray, and he'll always say yes. That prayer is, "God be merciful to me a sinner, save me, for Christ's sake." He will always say yes to that. St. Peter says, "He is not willing that any should perish, but that all should come to repentance."

I know Jesus will answer that prayer. He tells us that in Revelation 3:20: "I stand at the door and knock." He says, "Behold!" When he says "Behold," then you better pay attention and look, because it's an exclamation mark. "Behold, I stand at the door and knock. If anyone hear my voice and open the door, I will come in and sup with him." That is, we have fellowship with him, and live with him, and he with us.

I remember one day over seventy years ago, at Camp Judson in South Dakota, I was talking to one of the junior high boys and I gave him this verse. He wanted to accept Jesus, and he asked me something nobody has ever asked me since. That boy said, "What if I ask him to come in and he doesn't come in or he won't come in?" Never had I ever been asked before, but Jesus answered that and this is what I told him. Jesus says, "I will come in. If you open the door, I will come in." That's one prayer Jesus always answers, God always answers with a resounding yes.

The last thing I see here is that Lazarus became a witness, and many believed, and Christians were encouraged. That's what the new life is all about—to be a witness for Jesus Christ and to honor his name and glorify his name. Let's be like Lazarus and stand up and make a difference in this poor old world.

Heavenly Father, what a wonderful, wonderful story. We're thrilled as we read it. Only you could do it. Thank you that you did. I just pray that many today will call upon the name of the Lord and be saved, because they have no hope outside of Jesus. Thank you in Jesus's name. Amen.

PART III

The Love of Jesus

THE LORD IS MY SHEPHERD

Psalm 23

The LORD is my shepherd;
I shall not want.
He makes me to lie down in green pastures;
He leads me beside the still waters.
He restores my soul;
He leads me in the paths of righteousness
For His name's sake.
Yea, though I walk through the valley of the shadow of death,
I will fear no evil;
For You are with me;
Your rod and Your staff, they comfort me.
You prepare a table before me in the presence of my enemies;
You anoint my head with oil;
My cup runs over.
Surely goodness and mercy shall follow me
All the days of my life;
And I will dwell in the house of the LORD
Forever.

I DON'T KNOW HOW MANY TIMES I'VE BEEN ASKED TO preach on Psalm 23. Probably more than on any other passage. At funerals, or with people who are desperately sick or the shut-ins, Psalm 23 is often the requested Scripture. Sometimes people will ask for John 3:16, sometimes Psalm 27, sometimes Psalm 40, a lot of times, John 14. But by far and away, the most requested is the Twenty-Third Psalm.

This is a special psalm to me, because I was raised on a farm out in western South Dakota, ten miles west of Belle Fourche. And we didn't have irrigation, and we seldom had rain. We used to joke about it during the Depression. These ranchers and farmers were a special stock of people. And I'm part of them, that's why I say that. But they would joke around, and they'd say, "We had a three-inch rain," and they meant that we had a drop every three inches. Those were hard years, back in the thirties. We lost our farm in those years, so it wasn't easy going.

Psalm 23 means so much to me because I was raised on a farm, and my father always had sheep. The story of feuding between sheep men and the cattle men, there's a lot of truth to that. The sheep men didn't like the cattle men, and the cattle men didn't like the sheep men, and they didn't make any bones about it. But my dad always had the sheep.

Psalm 23 is a story about the shepherd and the sheep. David wrote this psalm, and he begins by saying, "The Lord is my shepherd."

Of course, David didn't know about Jesus, because Jesus hadn't yet been born of the virgin. David just knew that God was a kind and a loving God. Now a lot of people think of God as just the opposite. They think he's a terrible, mean, and cruel God who likes to torment and hurt people. Now, it's true that he's a God of justice, and he's going to deal in justice. But he's also a God of love. The great attribute of God is that he is a God of love.

David knew this about God. But when Jesus came, he tells us (in the tenth chapter of John's Gospel), "I am the good shepherd." He said, "The good shepherd giveth his life for the sheep. I lay it down, I have power to take it again. I received this commandment from the Father. And I have that power to raise myself from the grave." Which he did. And so we can say, "Jesus is my shepherd." We can say that because Jesus says, "He that has seen me has seen the Father."

In other words, if you want to know what God is like, just get to know Jesus, read about Jesus, study about Jesus. Because Jesus says, "I am God and I represent God and I am God in the flesh." So Jesus is my shepherd.

When David talks about a shepherd, there's a lot more to that than what appears on the surface. Because in America we just drive sheep from one pasture to another. We get some tin cans and bang them together, or we could get a sheep dog and chase the living daylights out of those poor sheep, and we drive them from one place to another. That was never how it was in the Middle East with David. He always led his sheep.

Remember what Jesus said: "My sheep hear my voice and I know them and they follow me." Then Jesus said it in another time, a little bit later: "A stranger they will not follow"—because they don't know that stranger. But when we know Jesus, we follow him; the sheep follow the shepherd.

I've seen that in the Middle East, while visiting my relatives in Lebanon. At the close of the day, you'll see these little bands of sheep—maybe five or ten, or maybe some fifty or more. They're all following their shepherd. And there's a space between them. They come right into the village, and they stay in the village right next to the house where the shepherd lives with his family.

The sheep follow the shepherd, and the shepherd loves the sheep and will die for his sheep. The story of the ninety and nine is a true story. If one sheep is out alone in the wild, the shepherd will go and find that sheep. He does it for two reasons. He does it, first of all, because he loves that sheep. And that's the way Jesus loved us. He loved us and gave himself for us. The second reason he goes out and finds that sheep is because his reputation is at stake.

If a shepherd discovered that one of his sheep was out in the wild, and he didn't go and look for that sheep, he'd be the talk of all the shepherds. He'd be a disgrace to the profession. They would look down on him because he didn't go and look for his sheep.

So Jesus is that wonderful shepherd. And where did he find you? Where did he find me? He came after us, and he came for us, and he called us to come to him. And we came to him, we put our trust in him. He's a wonderful, wonderful shepherd who leads us.

I remember reading a story of a tourist traveling in the Middle East, and the guide had just told him about how the sheep will always follow the shepherd, that he never drives them. And as they were going through one of the cities near Jerusalem, they saw a man driving his sheep. So they called this to the attention of the guide right away. They said, "Look over there—it's a shepherd driving his sheep." And the guide says, "No, that's not the shepherd, that's the butcher."

There's a whole lot of difference, because Jesus has us at heart. And the sheep know the difference. Even children know if you love them or not. You don't fool people. You can fool some for a little while, but they know whether you really love, and whether you really care. It's got to be genuine.

Jesus really cares. He's a wonderful shepherd, and he knows all about us. He knows every time you're discouraged. He knows every time you've got a tough decision to make. He knows every time you're downhearted. You may have had some tough roads; you may even now be having a hard time health-wise. You may be shut indoors, and you can't get out, you can't get around. But God knows all about that. He's touched with our infirmities. He's not a God that's away off yonder, who made us and then abandoned us. He's a God who made us and who dwells with us, because he *wants* to dwell with us. He dwells in the hearts and the lives of those who trust Jesus. He's a wonderful shepherd.

So David said, "I shall not want." You have to be careful about that, because what he means by "want" is that God is going to supply everything we have to have. And you know what we could live on. I don't even like to talk about it, because there's nothing I like better than good groceries. But you know, we could live on just bread and water. We could exist on bread and water alone. So anything we have beyond bread and water is a wonderful gift of this wonderful God. Sometimes we say, "Well, I want this and I want that," but it isn't for our good.

I remember years ago, out in Belle Fourche, we had a family that came to church and they were so poor. They had a terrible car, and half the time we had to help them get it started to go back home. Their car didn't have windows in it, and it was a windy bad day. We did the same thing on some of our cars; you had to hold up cardboard, and if the wind was from your side, you held up the cardboard all the way home. That's the way we traveled. You didn't look at the scenery, you held up your cardboard. And if you didn't, somebody would whack you, because you'd freeze to death. There were no heaters in those cars that amounted to anything.

So this family that would come to church had an awful car. We prayed that they get a better car, and they did get a better car, a nice car, but then they kept missing church. We didn't see them anymore, because they went driving every Sunday in their better car. So we were sorry we prayed that they got a better car. Sometimes we ask for things that are just not for our good, and you know that in your own lives.

David then talks about this wonderful Jesus, once he becomes your shepherd. And see, he becomes our shepherd when we put our faith in him. He's not our shepherd until we come to him, and confess our sins, and ask him to come into our hearts. Then we become the sheep of his flock, and he becomes our shepherd, and he leads us. David says, "He maketh me lie down on the green pastures, he leadeth me beside the still waters." That's the daily walk with the Lord.

I accepted the Lord when I was about ten years old in a country school house in western South Dakota. And Jesus has been with me ever since. A lot of times I haven't walked with him, a lot of times I've been unfaithful, a lot of times I've done wrong things, but he has never turned his back on me, never let me down.

He'll do the same thing with you. And when we make a mistake, when we commit a sin, he'll feel bad about it. The Holy Spirit will be grieved, and we just go to him and tell him that we're sorry. God will forgive us. He wants to have that fellowship with us. So he leads us.

Now, he directs our way, and I have a firm conviction that God has a plan for every Christian. He has something just for you to do. You may say, "Well, I'm a nobody, I don't have any money, I don't have any education, I don't have any talents I know of, and I'm just a loser." But don't you say that, because I don't care who you are or how young or old you are, and I don't care what you have. God has a plan for you. And you are very, very important in his body and in his kingdom.

When we accept the Lord, we become a part of his body. And that's a very important thing. Every part of my body is very, very important to me, except maybe a little excess weight, but I don't mind that even too much, because I made it a part of me. And you are a part of the body of Christ that makes that body function and do what it should do. So don't look down and say, "Well, there's no place for me in the church, there's no place for me in the kingdom." There's a place for you, and he will lead us if we let him.

So how does he lead us? We just have to submit to him. I think that one of our big problems is that we ask God to guide us, but we have certain bounds that we're not willing to go beyond. When we want God to guide us, we have to just give him everything, and then he'll show us and he'll lead us.

David says, "He leadeth me beside the still waters." Then he says, "He restoreth my soul." That is, he saves our soul through his work on the cross. And then, "He leadeth me in the paths of righteousness for his name's sake." Now that means that God starts to deal with us when we become his children. And the writer of the book of Hebrews says that God chasteneth every son that he receives. So God starts to deal with us. Sometimes he spanks us.

Dr. Spock wrote a book called *Baby and Child Care*. He sold more than 43 million copies. And the only bad thing was that he wrote it after I'd been raised, because my mother didn't have Dr. Spock's book on baby and child care. Dr. Spock said that parents should not resort to corporal punishment to correct them, that you should not spank them anywhere or anytime.[12] And if my mother would have had that book, it would have saved me a lot of grief, but she didn't have that book. Unfortunately, she had the Bible, and the Bible says, "Spare the rod and spoil the child." Mother believed that. So we got a whacking every once in a while.

Not long ago, I remember reading a news story by some researchers who determined that spanking may not be harmful to a child's health. They reported that a number of researchers have gone to great lengths in recent years to distinguish between the responsible use of disciplinary spanking and the kind of abusive physical punishment that Spock and others have rightly criticized.

If you have small children now, you wouldn't touch that little soul, but you know, as you grow older, God needs to correct us, and parents need to discipline a little bit. Now I'm not going to tell you when and what, but I'm just telling you that Spock raised a whole generation of kids that are out of control. And God doesn't do that because he leads me in the paths of righteousness. And when I go wrong, God deals with me. His Holy Spirit convicts us of a sin. Sometimes he has to put us in a hard place to make us look up.

I know a man who became so ill that they thought he was going to die. They rushed him to the Mayo Clinic, and he lived. When he came back he said, "My sickness was the most wonderful thing in the world, because it made me look up to God." He became a deacon in his church out in Wyoming, and he served the Lord for years and years, and then went to be with the Lord.

God does deal with us. So the next time you have a problem, all you need to do is say, "Now, dear Lord, is there something I need to be correcting?"

Maybe there isn't. Maybe God just wants to help us so that we are more submissive to him. Maybe he just wants to put us in a hard place so we learn to trust him more. Experiencing hardship doesn't mean that there's something really wicked in your life. You always want to be careful that, when somebody gets sick, you don't say, "Well, I suppose you were sinning in secret, and nobody knew about it, and now you're sick." Don't say that.

The apostle Paul had a thorn in his flesh, and he was as godly a man as ever was. When people suffer it doesn't mean that they were doing something wrong. Jesus suffered terribly, and he had no sin. So don't be putting that charge on somebody else. Just look in your own heart and say, "Dear Lord, is there something I ought to be correcting? Something I ought to be changing? What do you want to teach me in this problem?" And he will lead us in the paths of righteousness for his name's sake, because we're Christians, and we carry his name.

Then David goes on, and in the fourth verse of this psalm he says, "Yea, though I walk through the valley of the shadow of death, I will fear no evil, for thou art with me; thy rod and thy staff, they comfort me."

Now you know, we're all coming to death. A lot of people don't like to talk about death, especially young people. And that's all right, because death is the farthest thing from your mind. I remember going to a funeral for one of my classmates in high school. I was a pallbearer. As a young person, a teenager, I remember how reprehensible death was to me, how terrible. But you know, when you get to know Jesus and you get to trust Jesus, and when you get a few years on you, you know that you're going to come to that day, and you don't have to be afraid.

David says, I'm going to die, and I am not afraid. He said, "Yea, though I walk through the valley of the shadow of death, I will fear no evil; I am not afraid." Why would he not be afraid? "Because thou art with me, my shepherd is with me, Jesus is with me."

Husbands and wives would like to go together. I've had services for little children when the parents would have gladly gone with that child. When you come to the valley of the shadow of death, Jesus will be there. I remember one time I had a service for a darling little child, a little baby. And the mother said, "I just prayed and prayed that God would send an angel to help this little one over." And she said to me, "Do you think God did that?" "Oh," I said, "God did something a lot better than that. He sent Jesus."

If you don't know the Lord today, you should fear death. You should be afraid. But when you know Jesus, you know that when we get to death, he's going to be there. And I'm convinced that when we come to die, Jesus gives us special grace and special strength. In a special way, he's there.

I've seen so many people die, and I've seen them go quietly and joyfully without any struggle at all. And it's because Jesus gives special grace and strength. He doesn't give it ahead of time. I think that's what happens when spouses die or children die. I think God gives special grace.

Think of some of the tough things you've gone through in life. Wasn't God just special to you? Didn't he help you? If they would have told you ahead of time that this tragedy was going to happen to you—that you were going to go bankrupt, or your child would be taken from you, or something like that—you would say, "I couldn't handle it, I couldn't stand it." But God gives you special strength. If you're going to have cancer, I think God just gives you a special strength. He just helps you. So it doesn't scare you at all.

When I come to the valley of the shadow of death, David said, "The Lord Jesus, that good shepherd, he's right there; he'll take my hand." We're always a little nervous about experiences that are new experiences, aren't we? And we've never experienced death. I know we hear about these people that die and come back to life again. Now, I guess if I wanted to make some money, that's what I'd do—I would die and come back to life again, and then write a book about it and sell a bunch of copies. But I don't believe in that. After death comes the judgment—we meet God, and he settles it all.

So when we come to that last day, the Lord is right there, and he takes us through the valley of the shadow of death. I don't stay in that valley, I don't live in it, and I'm not afraid of it; it just takes me right to that wonderful Lord.

And where does he take us? David says, "You prepare a table before me in the presence of mine enemies." Then we come to that last beautiful verse. "Surely goodness and mercy shall follow me all the days of my life, and I will dwell in the house of the Lord forever." That's the end of walking with Jesus, that wonderful, wonderful place, so wonderful that it can't be put into words. No one could ever fully describe it.

Have you ever had feelings of something so wonderful? Well, try to describe a sunset so that a blind person hearing that story of a sunset could see it. We can't do it. In the same way, we can't tell about heaven. It's just too wonderful. It's just too beautiful. And it's for those who know the Lord, but you have to have Jesus. You have to have Jesus.

I remember reading a story about a king in medieval times, and he had a great feast to celebrate a certain anniversary. He had his whole kingdom come, and they had the biggest banquet you ever saw, and everybody was rejoicing and happy. During that feast, the king said to one of his servants, "There's a very famous orator here. He's known throughout the whole kingdom. Would you bring him up and have him come and give a quotation? Have him say something. I would just love to hear him." And the servant brought this orator up, and the orator recited the Twenty-Third Psalm. When he was done, everyone applauded and applauded. Then they went on with their banquet.

Pretty soon the king noticed an old pastor. And he said to his servant, "Have that old pastor come up. I want to honor him. I want him to say his few words." And the old pastor got up—and he also recited the Twenty-Third Psalm. When he finished, there was no applause—but there was scarcely a dry eye.

After it was all over, the king beckoned the orator, and he said to him, "How is it, with all of your degrees and all your training and travel and experience, that you couldn't move people at all like that old village preacher? Explain that to me." And the orator said, "It's because I know the psalm, but he knows the shepherd."

You know, there's a lot of people who read this psalm and they love it, but it doesn't mean a thing to them. And it's not for them. It's not for everybody. In the Twenty-Third Psalm, the key is given in the very first line: "The Lord is my shepherd." And if the Lord is just a great, wonderful shepherd, this isn't your psalm. But if the Lord Jesus is *your* shepherd—then this psalm is yours.

So how do we have him be our shepherd? Just call upon his name. "Whosoever will call upon the name of the Lord shall be saved."

I've met with people who tell me, "I don't know what to say. I don't know how to pray. I was never taught." Just think of it as talking to God. Just talk to God, and tell him that you're a sinner, and ask him to come into your heart and to save you.

When we were in an old church in downtown Aberdeen, South Dakota, I remember a young man there named Robert. He would say, "Well, God, I'm down here at Sixth and Lincoln"—as though God didn't know where he was. He told God where he was, and asked God to save him. That's all God wants to know.

He just wants you to say, "Yes, I want Jesus as my Savior." You just talk to him and say, "Dear God, I know I'm a sinner. I know I've done a lot of things wrong, and I know I should have done things that I didn't do. And I know I can't go to heaven with my sins. I know you died on the cross for my sins, I just ask you to come into my heart and take away my sin."

That's all. You don't have to have any special words. And you know, some who pray this prayer will immediately be very happy, and others won't feel anything. But you call on the name of the Lord, and you're saved.

So you just pray and ask Jesus to come into your heart, and you trust him, and you get out your Bible. Start reading the Bible. Read the book of John, or read the book of Romans. Don't read the Old Testament for a while. It's got some good stories in it, all wonderful stories, but start in the Gospel of John or in Romans. Just love the Lord. Get into church, get some Christian friends, and that wonderful, wonderful Lord will be your Lord and your shepherd.

Dear Lord Jesus, maybe there's somebody reading this right now who doesn't belong to you, but they want to. They know that you have come that they might have eternal life. And they know that you can't give that eternal life to them unless they ask for it. And you want to come into their heart, but you can't come into their heart unless they ask you to. I just pray every such person today will say, "Yes, I want Jesus, I want eternal life." Help them to come and receive you. And we'll give you all the thanks and praise, in Jesus's wonderful name. Amen.

JESUS, OUR
BURDEN BEARER

Matthew 11:28-30

Come to Me, all you who labor and are heavy laden, and I will give you rest. Take My yoke upon you and learn from Me, for I am gentle and lowly in heart, and you will find rest for your souls. For My yoke is easy and My burden is light.

THE APOSTLE PAUL TELLS US THAT WE HAVE ALL THINGS in Christ. If you have Jesus Christ, you are fully equipped, and in him you will have everything you need. This wonderful friend is here to help us. He isn't just a theory, but he actually literally helps those who trust him.

He gave us a great promise in Matthew 11, when he said, "Come unto me, all ye that labor and are heavy laden, and I will give you rest. Take my yoke upon you, and learn of me, for I am meek and lowly in heart, and you shall find rest unto your souls, for my yoke is easy, and my burden is light."

"Come unto me," Jesus says. And my dear friend, he's giving that as an invitation, and he's giving that invitation to all people, because he loves us. He went to the cross, he suffered and bled and died, he was raised on the third day—and he did all that so that he could say to us, "Come unto me." He did that so he can be the Savior of all the world. And he will save all who come unto him.

You understand that you could never meet God in your sins. God hates sin. We have so much injustice in this world, and we have so much sin in this world, that we kind of get used to it being around us. But it's something like being just a little bit warmer all the time, and we don't realize that the heat is being turned up until we're burned.

We live in a world filled with injustice, and we overlook sin so many times, we just let it go, and we think, "Well, that isn't so bad. It'll work out." But God must punish sin. There's some things that God cannot do, and he cannot countenance sin. He will not. We may put up with it in this world, and we may put up with sin in our life and in our church, but God will not do that. And that's all there is to it.

Jesus came so that he could say, "Come unto me, and I will help you out of this predicament, and I'll save you from this problem." He could say this, because he's God. Imagine if Peter or James or John or any of the apostles would say, "Come unto me, and I will take away your sins"—they wouldn't dream of saying such a thing. Only Jesus could say that. And he alone could say it because he's God, and because he died, and was buried, and raised the third day. So he's victorious over death.

He opened the way so that we can come to God. The veil of the temple was ripped down the middle. That wasn't some little flimsy cloth that they had in the temple in Jerusalem. Some of the Bible scholars tell us that this veil was very heavy, that it weighed maybe up to a hundred pounds. But when Jesus died it was torn down the middle, because the death of Jesus opened up the way so that people have access to God.

There used to be a day that no man could go beyond that veil except the high priest. And he could go only once a year, and he would represent the people. That veil was torn apart, and God came, his Son came, and made that possible. So Jesus tells us, "Come unto me, and you don't have to have a mediator."

Jesus never turned anyone away. When you read in the New Testament, you never find Jesus turning anybody away. There were people who left Jesus, but they did it on their own accord. It was never because he closed the door.

He'll never close the door on you. "Come unto me," he said, and you know that until you come to Jesus, you will never find redemption, and you'll never get rid of your burdens and the thing that bothers you.

The prodigal son would have died in that pigpen if he hadn't finally come to his senses, and that's what the Bible tells us. He came to himself, he came to his senses. He got something in his cranium, and he went to his father, and he found forgiveness, and he found the feast, and he found everything he'd been looking for earlier on his own in that far off country. He had it right there at home. When you come to Jesus as a prodigal, he'll help you.

"Come unto me," he says, and when we come to him we come to a person. We've got to be careful. I love the church, and I believe in baptism. Everybody ought to be baptized. Jesus says that he wants us to believe and be baptized. That's a commandment, but that'll never save you. And I believe you ought to be a member of a church, and you ought to love a church, and support the church. And if you don't like the church, you ought to find another you can like, and where you can serve, instead of snorting around all the time and complaining.

These are all important. The church is important, membership is important, baptism is important—but these are not salvation. Salvation is a person. "Come unto me," Jesus says. All these things have their place, but Jesus Christ is the key to it all.

So who was to come? Well, Jesus told us who was to come. He says, "Come unto me, all ye that labor and are heavy laden." He says "*all* ye"— no one is excluded. Sometimes I hear people say, "Oh, I've sinned too much. God would never have the likes of me." There's no one sinned but what God's grace will forgive—his wonderful, wonderful grace. He says,

"My grace is sufficient for you." And Paul tells us in the book of Romans, "Where sin abounded, God's grace did much more abound."

So you're not out of bounds, and you haven't committed the unpardonable sin. You can come if you want to, but the invitation of Jesus is to "all ye."

Then Jesus talked about a heavy burden. Think of the heavy burdens that some people have. Maybe you have a heavy load. You have a load of sin, and maybe it's bothering you, sins of the past. Maybe you have this sin of temptation, and you're tempted, though you decided you'd never do it again. You fall every time it raises its ugly head. You're having a problem with being tempted and falling.

Maybe it's sickness. All of a sudden, that sickness is thrust upon you. Maybe you had a stroke, and before that you were able to get up and around, but you can't do that now. Maybe it's poverty—maybe you lost your job. Maybe you've got bills you can't pay. Believe me, that hurts. That's heavy stuff. I know what that's like, to have bills that you can't pay, and you pay a little here and a little there.

Maybe it's weariness. Maybe you're tired of the struggling with life. Maybe it's discouragement. Maybe you just feel like you want to give up. We all have that.

I got a letter recently from one of the members of our church. He said, "I'm writing this letter just to encourage you." Believe me, that's one letter I'm not going to throw away. I might even spend money and get that thing framed. Encouragement. Nothing is so terrible as discouragement. The devil loves to discourage people. If he can get you discouraged, you'll be no value to the Lord or the church.

Maybe you'll just sit there, and you'll just worry. And maybe you have some big things to worry about, but God can take that worry away.

Maybe you've got heartache. Maybe you were in love with somebody. You were sure that was the person. I've seen that more than once, with young people especially. They think they're going to die. They don't die, but they think they're going to. Or maybe it's a divorce, a broken heart from a divorce, or from the loss of a loved one. Maybe you have sorrow nobody knows about. Maybe you're anxious about tomorrow, or you have remorse about your past. It could be a hundred different things. Maybe I haven't even mentioned it.

Or maybe it's declining health. Old age comes, and things don't work the way they used to. You've got some aches and pain in places you didn't even know you had before. They're showing up, and you're buying liniment as fast as you can. I heard about one old guy who married a young thing, and when people asked him about it, he said, "Well, I wanted to smell perfume and not liniment."

God knows your burden, whatever it is. He knows *you*, as you read this. It doesn't matter who you are, he knows you more perfectly than you know yourself. He knows the hairs of your head; he knows every teardrop you have.

So this wonderful Lord says, "Come," and he says, "I will give you rest." That's emphatic. He says, "I am going to do something. I'm not going to just give you some advice, and I'm not going to tell you just to have a stiff upper lip." Jesus comes, and he actually says, "I will give you rest." But we have to go to him. He's not going to give it to you till you go to him, till you get to him and confess your sins, and ask him to come into your heart, and you cast your cares upon him because he cares for you. That's what the Scripture says. Jesus is saying, "I am a person; come unto me, a person." It's a personal relationship. It's not something you read, some theory you get out of a book, some formula that you find. But you come to a person. And look what he says: "I will give you rest."

This doesn't mean we're going to sit under some shade tree and just twiddle our thumbs until he takes us home. It's not that at all. It doesn't mean that we won't have things to do. We are never saved to sit, we are saved to serve, every one of us.

You say, "Well, I don't have much education." That doesn't matter. You say, "I don't have much faith, I'm not a very strong Christian." It doesn't matter. Even if you're a child, it doesn't matter.

Remember the story of Naaman, where a little girl who was a slave revealed how God could heal a leper. A little girl was the key to the salvation of the commander in chief of the Syrian army! He went back to Damascus, and he even hauled dirt from down in Israel. He hauled donkey loads full of dirt to build himself a place there, where he could worship the God of Israel on the soil of Israel. How many people have come to Christ because of a little girl?

If you're a child at home, you get to work and get your folks to church. Maybe your mom already goes to church, but your dad just sits at home like a bump on a log. Talk to him and tell him to come to your church with you. You beg him, and you nag him. Your mother can't nag him, he just gets more stubborn—like an old goat, sitting there in his old rocking chair before the TV, until God pulls him out of this world, and he goes to a Christless eternity. But you can just hound him to death, and drive him nuts, and get him to church. All of us need to be doing that, and all of us have to serve. There's a place for every one of us.

Remember Adam and Eve in the garden of Eden? Adam had to work. God took him and put him in the garden of Eden to dress it and keep it. That's what he did. He didn't just sit there and smell the flowers. He worked in the garden of Eden.

And you know what Jesus says to the faithful worker in Matthew 25. Jesus didn't tell the man, "You've been faithful in a few things, now you get to retire." No, this is what he said: "Well done, good and faithful servant. You've been faithful over a few things, I'll make thee ruler over many things." He was saying, "I'll give you more work!" One of the most wonderful things in the world is being able to work. Those people who are sitting around looking wise—they're not happy.

"So take my yoke upon you," Jesus says, "learn of me." We're to take his yoke upon us. His yoke refers to the service that Christ gives us to do. When he talks about a yoke, he means service. "I'm going to give you some work to do. I'm going to take this heavy burden you can't handle, and I'm going to give you something to do, and you can work and carry on."

"Learn of me," Jesus said, and that's what we're doing. That's what we do when we read the Bible, and have Christian friends, and read Christian books, and watch Christian movies and such as that. Learn of him. You can never get too much of Jesus.

Jesus says, "Because I'm meek and lowly in heart." That's what he wants us to do. Learn to be meek. It simply means to be humble, and not to think of ourselves more highly than we ought, and not to look down on anybody ever.

The worst thing in the world is a holier-than-thou attitude. God just shudders when he sees that. Some of the harshest words, maybe the harshest words Jesus ever spoke, are the words he gave the Pharisees, who felt they were so much more spiritual and better than other people. God just hates that attitude.

"Lowly in heart"—that's Jesus. And we read in Philippians, "In lowliness of mind let each esteem others better than himself." Just give yourself to the Lord.

And then Jesus says this: "Ye shall find rest unto your souls." When we come to him and we take his burden, we find rest unto our souls. That's one thing the world doesn't have. They don't have rest.

Look wherever you want, watch any television show you want, there's always war somewhere. And Jesus said, "There will be wars and rumors of wars, until the Son of God comes again." The world doesn't have peace, and the world doesn't have rest. So Jesus says, "Take my yoke upon me, learn of me, be meek, and lowly." And if you do that, "Ye shall find rest unto your souls."

In verse 28, he says, "I will give you rest." And in verse 29, he says, "Ye shall find rest." He'll give you rest, you'll find rest. They are not the same. When he says, "I will give you rest," he's saying, "I will give you my righteousness, so that you don't worry about those sins. I'll wash them away in my blood. I'm going to give you that peace, I'm going to give you that rest."

We never find rest until we separate ourselves, and begin this service for Christ. That's where we get our rest. The rest that he gives us, that's *justification*. The rest that you find, that's *sanctification*—separating ourselves to the Lord.

Jesus says, "My yoke is easy, my burden is light." What did he mean by easy? The Greek word for that is a word that means, "well fitting." So you could say that the yoke of Jesus fits each of us well.

Now, when Jesus said this, every Palestinian knew what he was talking about, when he talked about a yoke. He was talking about oxen, and you put this yoke on the oxen's shoulder, and then the oxen will work for you.

That wooden yoke was very important. They would come to the carpenter shop to have a wooden yoke made. And the carpenter would take measurements. They came from miles to a good carpenter, and then he would measure that animal, and he would make the yoke for it, and make alterations as necessary. That's the way they worked to craft those yokes for the oxen. They measured each ox, and they measured those yokes. And then, after it was ready, the man would bring these oxen back, and they would try it on, they would fit it, like a bride fits her gown. And so it goes. You may ask, "Why did they have to be so careful?"

Well, I was raised out on the farm, and I'm proud of it. We used to do a lot of work with the horses. And when you would have a horse, you would have to harness a horse. The first thing you put on was the collar. The collar went around the neck. Young people today don't know if you hang a horse's collar on the neck or the tail, but you put the collar around the neck.

The horse really doesn't pull the load, but he pushes the load. He pushes on that collar, and that pulls the load. Now, if that collar doesn't fit, that horse will get a sore. He'll get a big boil there, and he can't push against that. I've seen that happen. When you get a horse that gets that sore on his shoulder, you put him out to pasture till it heals.

Now what Jesus is talking about here is this: "I'm going to give you a well-fitting yoke, I'm going to give you a well-fitting job. I'm going to put you in my service, I'm going to give you service that fits you perfectly." Because he knows all about us. He knows what talents we have, he knows what gifts he's given us. He knows everything about us. He knows all about me. He gave me a yoke that fits me perfectly, because I'm happy in his service, and I'm going to serve him in some place till I drop dead.

I'm going to serve. It isn't a drudgery, it isn't a terrible thing. I love to go to work. Now that's what he has for you, this wonderful Jesus.

By the way, there's a legend that says Jesus, over his carpenter shop in Nazareth, had a sign that said, "My yokes fit well." And the word got around, and they brought those oxen for miles and miles to Jesus of Nazareth to make their yoke. I don't know if that's true, but I do know that if you give your life in service for Christ, he will fit you with perfect service that brings you joy.

If you give your life to Jesus, you'll find out that his yoke is easy, that his yoke is good, that his yoke is serviceable. It's something you can do. You can't do what I am doing, and I can't do what you're doing, because every one of us has some custom-made yoke for service. "Take my yoke," Jesus says, "I'll custom-make it, just for you."

When he talks about his yoke being easy, he doesn't mean that there won't be battles and struggles and trials. Jesus never fooled anybody into following him.

Listen to what he says in Matthew 16. Jesus said to his disciples, "If any man will come after me, let him deny himself." That's tough business, to deny yourself. That's why I don't go on a diet very often—I don't like to deny myself. But Jesus says, "Let him deny himself, and take up his cross." That's no fun. But that's what Jesus said: "You want to be my disciple, you got to deny yourself, take up your cross. You got to follow me."

As the days go by, and we labor for him, and we have our battles and our troubles, and our trials and our struggles, we have a wonderful peace.

We know that God's going to take care of these things. All these burdens we give to him, we just get busy serving him. And if you don't serve the Lord, then you're not going to be happy. You've got to be active in the Lord's work. Because if you're not, you won't be happy in life. You'll just be a problem to yourself and for everybody around you. So get busy for Jesus.

Jesus says, "Now come to me, receive me as your Savior. And you'll take this yoke, you take this pattern I have for you." God has a pattern of life for everyone, whether you're young or you're old.

He's still got a plan for you, even if you're tottering and ready to slip into the grave. He says, "You're going to bear fruit in old age." His plan for us doesn't quit when we reach sixty-five. His plan for us goes for as long as we breathe. And he says, "When you're done breathing, I'll take you home, and the plan is done."

Sure, there are struggles and trials. Do you think the devil is going to stand by and let you give your life to Christ without fighting you? He'll fight you every turn of the road. But with this wonderful yoke, this wonderful service, Jesus tells us, "Just take it."

We read in 1 John 5:3, "For this is the love of God, that we keep his commandments." And also this: "And his commandments are not grievous." The *Living Bible* states it this way: "Loving God means doing what he tells us to do, and really, that isn't hard at all."

So think of it this way: We're yoked with Jesus Christ, the Son of the living God. We're going to look upon his lovely face someday. We're going to see him in the flesh, going to talk to him. We're going to look upon him.

But right now, until that happens, we're yoked with Jesus. We're walking side by side with him, we're in the same business. What an honor, what a joy.

There was an Anglican bishop in the nineteenth century named J. C. Ryle, and he wrote,

> No doubt, there's a cross to be carried, if we follow Christ. No doubt, there are trials to be endured, and battles to be fought. But the comforts of the gospel far outweigh the cross, compared to the service of the world in sin, compared to the yoke of Jewish ceremonies, and the bondage of human superstition. Christ's service, is, in the highest sense, easy and light. His yoke is no more a burden than the feathers are to a bird. His commandments are not grievous. His ways are always pleasantness, and all his paths are peace.[13]

The yoke is the doing of God's will. The burden is the carrying of his cross. And so, we have to search ourselves, and we have to give ourselves.

G. Campbell Morgan, a great London preacher of another day, put it this way: "We must get to him, we must submit to him, and we must serve him."[14]

The centuries-old hymn "Fairest Lord Jesus" goes like this:

Fairest Lord Jesus, ruler of all nature,
O thou of God and man, the Son,
thee I will cherish, thee I will honor,
thou my soul's glory, joy, and crown.
Fair are the meadows, fairer still the woodlands,
robed in the blooming garb of spring.
Jesus is fairer, Jesus is purer,
who makes the woeful heart to sing.
Fair is the sunshine, fairer still the moonlight,
and all the twinkling starry host.
Jesus shines brighter, Jesus shines purer
than all the angels heaven can boast.
Beautiful Savior, Lord of the nations,

Son of God and Son of Man,
glory and honor, praise, adoration
now and forevermore be thine.

Receive Christ, confess Christ, and serve Christ.

Thank you, heavenly Father, for Jesus. Thank you that he loves us, and loved us so much that he died for us. I don't know anybody who would do that for me, but he did. Thank you that we can come to him and find relief and release from our troubles and trials. And we can make our life worth living and worthwhile by taking your yoke, and serving you. Help us all to do that. We pray in Jesus's name. Amen.

JESUS PRAYS
FOR US

John 17:12-19

While I was with them in the world, I kept them in Your name. Those whom You gave Me I have kept; and none of them is lost except the son of perdition, that the Scripture might be fulfilled. But now I come to You, and these things I speak in the world, that they may have My joy fulfilled in themselves. I have given them Your word; and the world has hated them because they are not of the world, just as I am not of the world. I do not pray that You should take them out of the world, but that You should keep them from the evil one. They are not of the world, just as I am not of the world. Sanctify them by Your truth. Your word is truth. As You sent Me into the world, I also have sent them into the world. And for their sakes I sanctify Myself, that they also may be sanctified by the truth.

WE ARE ENTERING INTO ONE OF THE MOST BEAUTIFUL chapters in all the Bible, the seventeenth chapter of John. When we come to this chapter, it's like walking on holy ground, and we feel like Moses at the burning bush. We ought to take off those sandals and stand in reverence.

G. Campbell Morgan says that in this chapter, "we are permitted to come into his presence, as under the very shadow of the cross, he held communion with his Father."[15]

Philip Melanchthon, one of the great church reformers and a contemporary of Martin Luther, said about this chapter, "There is no voice which has ever been heard, either in heaven or in earth, more exalted, more holy, more fruitful, more sublime than the prayer offered up by the Son of God Himself."

Warren Wiersbe also comments on this chapter, in these words:

It is the greatest prayer ever prayed on earth, and the greatest prayer recorded anywhere in Scripture. John 17 is certainly the holy of holies of the gospel record, and we must approach this chapter with a spirit of humility and worship. To think that we are privileged to listen in as God the Son converses with his Father, just as he is about to give his life as a ransom for sinners.[16]

So it's a beautiful, beautiful chapter, and this chapter really is the Lord's Prayer. There's another prayer that's really a model prayer. The disciples said, "Teach us to pray," and Jesus gave that model prayer. We call that the Lord's Prayer in Matthew 6, but that's just a model or a plan for prayer. John 17 is really the Lord's Prayer in every sense of the word. We get to see the heart of God as the Son and the Father commune with each other, when Jesus is only hours away from the cross. In less time that it takes to tell it, Jesus is going to be before Pilate, and he's going to go on to that cross.

So let's look at this chapter. It's divided into three sections. In the first section, Jesus prays for himself. In the second section, he prays for his disciples. And in the third section, he prays for the church. That's you and me today.

So let's look closer. In the first five verses, Jesus prays for himself. "Jesus spoke these words, lifted up his eyes to heaven, and said: 'Father, the hour has come. Glorify thy Son, that thy Son also may glorify thee.'" He's talking about the cross, and he's not talking about it as some hideous, terrible thing, but as a glorious thing. He says here, "Glorify thy Son. The hour has come. Glorify thy Son." He's talking about his death on the cross and also his resurrection.

The reason it's such a glorious thing to Jesus and to the Father in heaven is that this is the means of our salvation. If not for that cross and the subsequent resurrection of Jesus Christ, you and I would have no hope in this world or in the world to come, and we would spend our eternity with Satan and his demons.

So this is a glorious experience, and it's a terrible experience as we look upon his suffering. Yet to Jesus, it's a glorious thing, because he's going to open the gates of heaven for all the people that want to come in.

He says here, "The hour is come." We first heard him talk about this at the marriage at Cana of Galilee where he performed his first recorded miracle. Jesus said, "Mine hour has not yet come." He says that over and over. His hour hasn't come. They want to kill him. They want to stone him. They want to cast him over the cliff in Nazareth. He says, "My hour isn't come. It isn't ready yet."

But now he says, "The hour is come. The cross is here. It is ready. I'm ready to go." So Jesus prays for himself.

Now I don't think there's anything wrong with praying for yourself. I think we're very foolish if we don't because we need prayers. We pray for others, we ought to pray for ourselves. The only thing we have to be careful about is that we're always praying in the will of God, and that we aren't praying for some little selfish thing, but for the great glory of God.

So that's what Jesus does in the first verse. He says, "Glorify thy Son that the Son may glorify thee." So he's talking about the cross, and he's saying that he wants to be glorified in that cross so he can glorify the Father. It isn't for himself that he's seeking glory and praise and honor, although we give him that and rightly so. But he's doing this to glorify the Father in heaven.

I remember reading the story of Corrie ten Boom. She and her father and her family hid the Jews in Holland during World War II. Finally they were discovered, and they were sent to a concentration camp. Corrie's sister Betsie died in that concentration camp, but by a miracle, just a mix-up in orders, Corrie ten Boom was set free. It was purely the hand of God that set her loose.

She went all over the world talking about how she forgave those who killed her sister and forgave those who operated the concentration camp, and how she just was living for God and praising God. Corrie ten Boom says, "They give me a lot of compliments, and I take those compliments like I take a bouquet. Then at the close of the day, after I have all those compliments and all those bouquets, I just lift them up and say, 'Here, God, they belong to you.'"[17]

That's the way Jesus was living, and that's the way you and I need to live. We need to give all the glory to the Father in heaven. All that we do and all that we attempt and all that we say and all of our giving needs to be done for the glory of God.

Then Jesus said something else: "And now, O Father, glorify thou me with thy own self, with the glory which I had with thee before the world was." So Jesus now is not talking about the glory of the cross, but about the glory he had in heaven. There was never any beginning of that glory. He always had it, and he always will have it in the end. But there was a space of thirty-three years that he set it aside, when he was born of the virgin and lived among us, and his glory was in heaven, waiting for him.

Some Bible scholars say that when Jesus ascended into heaven and there was a great cloud that received him, he was receiving back his glory. That might've been. But at any rate, Jesus is praying that he can complete this work and that he can go and be with his Father in heaven and receive that glory.

Then he prays for his disciples, in verses 6-19. He says, "I have manifested thy name to them." That is, he had revealed much of God to them. They knew more about God than they'd ever known before, because they knew Jesus. They understood more about God, although there was a lot they didn't understand. But they understood a lot more because Jesus had manifested God's name, and that name stands for his character and his being, and he has shown them God.

They never would have seen God in the stars and the moon, though they could see his power and his might. They never see God out on the golf course or in the fishing boat. You have to come to Jesus, and have Jesus. You can see his wisdom and his beauty, but you can't see God till you see Jesus, and you see him in his Word.

Jesus prayed three things for these men. He says, first of all, "Keep them in thy name." Then he prays, "Keep them from evil." And then he prays, "Sanctify them in thy name, that they may be one."

"Keep them in thy name"—being kept in his name is accomplished when we keep from evil and we sanctify ourselves. We then are kept in his name. So the two tell us how to do the one.

Jesus said something very interesting here, too, here in John 17. In verse 9, he said, "I pray not for the world." You'll wonder immediately, "What is this, that he isn't praying for the world?" He says he loves the world, and he says he came to die for the world. Now he says, "I'm not praying for the world."

Well, God is never inconsistent, you can mark that down, and he's always right on. Jesus is simply saying here, "I want to win the world, but I want to win them through my people, my disciples, and later on my church, the body of Christ." He says, "Keep them in thy name that they may be one as we are one." He says that he's wanting those people to love him and be one and a witness, because he loves the world. But he's praying for his disciples, that through his disciples he can win the world.

Jesus never lost sight of a poor lost sinner. And if you're reading this, and you've never received Jesus Christ, know that God loves you, and he doesn't want you to go into hell. He wants you to be in heaven with him. So he has sent the church, and he sent witnesses, and he sent your neighbors who know the Lord and love the Lord, so that you can know about Christ and can come to Christ and believe.

Jesus said, "I pray not that thou should take them out of the world." He says to his Father, "I'm not praying for you to take them out of the world." Our business is in the world, because that's where the lost people are. So we need to live in this world. It doesn't mean that we go down at the bar and sit on some stool and try to witness. That's counterproductive.

But what it means is that when you go to school and when you go to work and when you get together for whatever reason—and you walk in this world and you have the contacts in this world—you do it knowing that we are in the world to witness, so that others can know Jesus Christ and believe on him and find everlasting life. He says, "I pray that you'll be one."

Jesus also says to his Father, "I pray that thou shouldst keep them from the evil one."

How would they be kept from the evil one? Jesus says, "Sanctify them." That's the way we're kept from the evil one. We are sanctified. Well, what does sanctify mean? It doesn't mean that you have a halo, and there's all kinds of lights shining out of your head, or anything like that. Charles Swindoll puts it this way: "The word *sanctify* is often misunderstood. It doesn't mean a halo or glowing spirituality. It means to be set apart for a certain purpose, for an intended use." And he says, "If you take food out of the refrigerator for dinner, then in the biblical sense, you've sanctified that food, set it apart for a specific use. It's sanctified."

The furniture in the tabernacle was sanctified. It was set apart. What God is saying here is, "I want my children, I want you disciples, to be set apart. Come out from among them. Live a life so that they can tell you're a Christian. Don't run with the dogs." We had an old evangelist who used to say, "If you run with the dogs, you're going to get fleas." We just have to live a separated life for the Lord. That's what sanctified means. So Jesus wants to win the world because his people are separated and witnessing for him. That's his prayer.

He says, "I'll tell you how you can be sanctified." He says in John 17:19, "And for their sakes I sanctify myself, that they also might be sanctified through the truth"—through the Word of God, through the Bible. That's the way it works, when we read the Bible. When we go to church where the Bible is preached, and when we get into Bible studies, and we go to Sunday school and read about the things of God and read the Word of God, we are sanctified. We're separated from the world. And then we'll know a false doctrine if we see it.

That's why the cults prosper so much. They can tell people anything, and people believe it. They could tell them that the moon is made out of green cheese, and some would actually believe it.

If you don't know what you stand for, you're going to fall for anything. So read the Bible, study the Bible, go where the Bible is preached, listen to sermons about the Bible, because the truth sanctifies us and sets us apart.

Then Jesus prays for the church, in verses 20-26 of John 17. And that's where you and I show up in this prayer. Jesus is praying for us in this prayer. When he prayed this prayer two thousand years ago, he saw your face. He saw my face. He saw the face of every believer who would ever trust him and believe in him.

He saw you. Jesus tells us, "Not a sparrow falls to the ground, but what the heavenly Father sees that and knows that." There are sparrows all over the world, countless sparrows. But when one little sparrow falls, the heavenly Father sees that.

And he knows the number of hairs on your head, and he's not just talking about bald-headed men here. If you lose one single hair, God not only sees you lose that hair, but he knows how many hairs are still on your head. Can you imagine that? We can't imagine or comprehend that.

God knows all about us, and he knows every heartache we have. He knows every yearning we have. He knows every temptation we have. He knows every weakness we have. But he loves us.

So as Jesus prays, he's looking down the corridor of time, and he sees today and he sees you reading this today. And he says, "I'm praying for you," in verse 20. He says, "Neither pray I for these alone," that is his disciples. He says, "I pray for them also, which shall believe on me through their word." He's looking down the corridors of time, and he sees all of these people—Luther, and Calvin, and Knox, and Moody, and Graham, and you and me and my children and your children and our grandchildren that trust Jesus. He sees them all.

He doesn't just look at a great big old world with a mass, a glob of humanity. But he looks at individuals, one and one and one. That's why he's such a wonderful God. That's why, when you talk to him, you are important to him, and he hears you and he loves you.

So he prays for these people called the church. He prays three things for his church. He prays first of all that they may be one, in verse 21. Second, in that same verse, he prays that the world may believe. And he prays third, in verse 24, that we'll be in heaven with him.

He says, "I pray that they might be one." Now God isn't talking about a universal world church here. I don't think he has that in mind at all. But he's looking at his believers all over the world who have the same purpose in mind, and that is to honor Jesus Christ and honor God the Father, and to win people to himself.

Charles Swindoll puts it this way:

When Jesus prays, it's not for uniformity of organization, style, personality, and appearance. Neither does he pray for unanimity, absolute agreement of opinion within a group of people. Nor does he pray for union, absolute coalition of or tight affiliation within the ranks of Christianity. What he does pray for is unity, oneness of heart, of faith, and of purpose. And that can be all different denominations all over the world.[18]

It might come as a surprise to some people, but there just might be some people up there in heaven besides the Baptists, and it might surprise some people that some of the Baptists may not make it. Because if we don't have our faith, we can go through all the motions, and we can be immersed, and all of the rest of it, and we can look really holy—but unless we have that faith in Jesus Christ, we have no hope in this world or the world to come.

Merrill Tenney, a great scholar, wrote this:

Within the church of historic Christianity, there have been wide divergences of opinion and ritual. Unity, however, prevails wherever there's a deep and genuine experience of Christ, for the fellowship of the new birth transcends all historical and denominational boundaries. Paul of Tarsus, Luther of Germany, Wesley of England, Moody of America would find deep unity with each other, though they were widely separated by time, by space, by nationality, by educational background, and by ecclesiastical connections.[19]

It's in Christ that we are one, and that's what brings us together. We aren't all going to see things the same way, but we can all love the same way, and we can all have our determination to serve Christ the same way.

Think about the disciples, these twelve men that Jesus had. Boy, did he have a conglomeration. Here was Matthew. Don't think that he wasn't a thick-skinned guy. He was a tax collector, and he didn't take no for an answer, and there he sits. Then there was Peter, and he's as impulsive as you can get. He's just like people you may be acquainted with, and you never know where they're going to jump next. Impulsive, self-confident, half-proud.

He's also got Thomas, and Thomas is wondering and he's doubting. He's never sure, and he's always questioning. What's he ever going to amount to?

He's also got James and John, and look at them—rough, tough fishermen. Jesus calls them Sons of Thunder. How'd you like them on your church's board of deacons?

Here they are, all this conglomeration, and they didn't see eye-to-eye on things at all. But they had one goal in mind, and that was to follow Jesus Christ. When Jesus Christ left, that coalition didn't fall apart, because the Holy Spirit came, the same Spirit that we have. He drew them together, and he bound them together, and they were one as they went out to witness for Christ and move on.

That's what we have to do in the church today. We have to bind together and not get upset over every little dumb thing that comes along. One pastor said his church members were just like a bunch of balloons, and he said, "I don't know which one's going to blow up next." Grow up, and don't blow up.

Jesus prayed also that the world might believe. The church is to be united, they're to be one, and in that way we can give a witness to the world. Jesus says here in John 17:18, "As thou has sent me into the world, even so have I also sent them into the world." As God sent the Son, and as the Son sent the disciples, so the Father sends us into the world. He sends us not on our own—one here and one there—but as a band, grouped together, loving and forgiving and moving on and learning to forgive. As Peter said, when we have real love for each other, it will overlook a multitude of sins or faults. You do that with your grandchildren; why not do it with people in the church?

Then look at the last thing. Jesus prayed for our eternal destiny. He says, "Father, I will that they also whom thou has given me, be with me where I am, that there they may behold my glory, which thou has given me, for thou has lovest me before the foundation of the world." Jesus speaks about those people that trust him, "whom thou hast given me." That is, every believer is a gift from God for the Son.

We are gifts to the Son, and God gives a gift that he never takes back, and we are secure in Christ. We are in his love. Jesus talks about his love. He says, "Before the foundation of the world, he loved me." We had that love before there ever was a world. We are included in that love, because we're in the love of God and the love of Christ when we receive his Son.

How can you ever worry about your eternity when you're that tied in with the love of God? We never have to worry. We never have to fret. You can worry if you want to, but it's a waste of time. We're saved, and we're saved forever when we come to Jesus and trust in him.

Paul put it this way (in *The Living Bible*):

Who then can ever keep Christ's love from us? When we have trouble or calamity, when we are hunted down or destroyed, is it because he doesn't love us anymore? And if we are hungry or penniless or in danger or threatened with death, has God deserted us No. No, for the Scriptures tells us that for his sake, we must be ready to face death at any moment of the day. We are like sheep awaiting slaughter. But despite all this, overwhelming victory is ours through Christ who loved us enough to die for us. For I am convinced that nothing can ever separate us from his love. Death can't, the angels won't, and all the powers of hell itself cannot keep God's love away. Our fears for the day, our worries about tomorrow, or where we are high above the sky or in the deepest ocean—nothing will ever be able to separate us from the love of God demonstrated by our Lord Jesus Christ when he died for us. (Romans 8:35-39)

So in this beautiful prayer in John 17, he's praying for us, praying for us today, all of us who trust him, all of us who put our faith in him. Jesus is praying that we'll be safe in this world, and that we'll witness, and that we'll shine—and that someday we'll be with him and see his glory and share in his glory.

That's what Jesus has prayed, and God will answer his prayer. So what we have to do is receive him and trust him and serve him. There's just nothing else that's logical, is there? Receive him and trust him and serve him.

Dear Lord, we do love you, and we are here because we love you and we trust you. But Lord, maybe somebody who is reading this has not yet received you into their life. Help them to do that this very moment. Help them just to pray, "God, be merciful to me, a sinner. Just save me, dear Lord. Come into my life." Help them to pray that in their own words, and then help us to rejoice in such a great Savior. We thank you that we belong to you and that you belong to us, and that we will never be torn asunder. In Jesus's name, we praise you. Amen.

LO, I AM
WITH YOU
ALWAYS

Matthew 28:18-20

And Jesus came and spoke to them, saying, "All authority has been given to Me in heaven and on earth. Go therefore and make disciples of all the nations, baptizing them in the name of the Father and of the Son and of the Holy Spirit, teaching them to observe all things that I have commanded you; and lo, I am with you always, even to the end of the age." Amen.

Today I'd like to give hope and encouragement to the people of God through the closing verses of Matthew 28 where Jesus said, "Go ye, therefore, and teach all nations, baptizing them in the name of the Father, and of the Son, and the Holy Spirit, and teaching them to observe whatsoever I have commanded you." Then Jesus said— and this is what I want to zero in on— "Lo, I am with you always, even unto the end of the age."

Jesus was able to make that wonderful promise, because he said, "All authority is given me in heaven and on earth." The source of authority is God's throne. It's not the government, and it's not some dictator, and it's not the forces of evil, and it isn't Satan. The one who will have the last word is God Almighty. He hasn't abdicated from the throne, and he never will. We can rest upon what he says. And when he says it, you can count on it: "Lo, I am with you always."

I read the story of G. Campbell Morgan. He was a great preacher in the early twentieth century in London. He's called the prince of expositors, and his writings, especially on the Gospels, are still used in Christendom. When G. Campbell Morgan was a young Christian, he used to visit several elderly ladies once a week to read the Bible to them. When he came to the end of Matthew's Gospel, Morgan read, "Lo, I am with you always, even unto the end of the age." He added, "Isn't that a wonderful promise?" One of the ladies quickly replied, "Young man, that is not a promise. It is a fact!"[20]

And there's a lot of truth to that. There are no conditions for us to meet. Jesus says to his people, "I'm with you always, whether you're good or bad." No conditions to meet. There isn't anything to do, but to believe. And the fact is, Jesus Christ is with us.

Paul found that to be true when he was in Corinth. He was starting a church in a cesspool, because Corinth was a terrible, immoral city. We think we have immoral cities today, but Corinth was just as bad or worse. And Paul proved something to us. He proved that you could walk right into the very pit of sin and establish a church, and win people to Jesus Christ, and break the power of the devil.

Paul was in Corinth, and he had some pretty tough going. But in a special vision, God came to him to encourage him, and said, "Be not afraid, for I am with thee." God always says that to his people.

He says it in a time of sickness. He says it when we resist having to go in a nursing home. He says it when we come to die. He says it when we're sorely tempted and we fail. He comes and tells us, "I'm with you. Don't you be afraid. I love you. I redeemed you, if you've received me as your Savior. And I'll be with you."

Warren Wiersbe puts it this way: "The phrase 'The end of the age' indicates that our Lord has a plan; he is the Lord of history." And Wiersbe goes on: "As the churches follow his leading and obey his word, they fulfill his purposes in the world. It will all come to a climax one day. Meanwhile, we must all be faithful."[21]

So God is with us. And there are many ways that he's with us.

He's with us first of all as my Savior, my Savior from sin. We make a big thing of that in our church, because if you die in your sin, you're going to hell. Jesus says, "I can't have any sin in heaven. And if you don't have that sin taken care of through the blood of Jesus Christ, there's no place in heaven for you."

Some people say, "I can't believe that God made hell for people." Well, God didn't make hell for people. God made hell for the devil and his angels. But if we align with Satan and his angels, and if we're in the kingdom of darkness, we spend eternity with the devil and his angels in that lake of fire that has no end.

We're talking about sin, being saved from sin, but there's another interesting point here. Jesus is my Savior from the sins that I commit day by day—and hour by hour, I might add, with some of us. Because every thought that is wrong is sin, and every failure to do what God wants us to do is sin. There are all kinds of sins, as God fully knows. But when he saves us, he washes us clean, and we're saved from all our sins—past, present, and future.

But while we walk this earth, we're defiled even as we try to walk in the pathway of light. So day by day we need a Savior to cleanse us on our earthly walk.

Jesus pointed that out very well in John 13, in his dealing with Peter. After they had eaten, Jesus got up from the supper table, took off his robe, and wrapped a towel around him. He poured water into a basin, and began to wash the disciples' feet and to wipe them with the towel he had around him.

When he came to Simon Peter, he said to Jesus, "Master, you shouldn't be washing our feet like this."

Jesus replied, "You don't understand now why I am doing it, but someday you will."

"No," Peter protested, "you shall never wash my feet."

"But if I don't, you have no part with me," Jesus said.

Simon Peter said—and this sounds just like him— "Wash my hands and head as well, not just my feet."

Then Jesus said, "One who has bathed all over needs only to have his feet washed to be entirely clean. Now you're clean, but that isn't true of everyone here." And he was talking about Judas at that point.

So Jesus is washing his feet, and Peter says, "Give me a whole bath." And the Lord says, "You don't need a whole bath. You've been cleansed by my blood. But I need to wash your feet." Now what's he saying? Jesus is saying that when we come to him, we're cleansed in the blood of Christ, and we have that full bath.

But in those days, they had public bathhouses, and they used to walk from that place to their residence. And while they walked that distance, there was dirt on the street, and they wore sandals, so they got their feet dirty. When they got to their church or their house or wherever they were going, they washed their feet. They'd already had their bath, so they washed just their feet, because their feet were all that was defiled.

When we walk through this life, we are defiled every day by our thoughts and our actions, and also by our inaction. We need a Savior to save us once and for all, and also to cleanse us daily, because without that daily cleansing, we don't have fellowship with God. When we sin, that fellowship gets cut off. Not our salvation, but our fellowship gets destroyed.

To restore that fellowship, we need to come to God and to Jesus, and be cleansed of that sin, to have our earthly life cleansed, and to walk with him. So we need him as a Savior. He's there as the Savior to save us and to help us day by day.

When Jesus says, "Lo, I am with you always," it means we have him with us as a shepherd. In this particular instance, we have a shepherd to guide us, a shepherd to guard us. There are so many things in this world that can hurt us, and not just physically. And there's something even more insidious—and that's the cults, and the false teachings, and the false doctrine.

The church had barely been born at Pentecost, when Satan already had a counterfeit faith and a counterfeit teaching. He was trying to lead people astray. That's why Paul wrote, and that's why John wrote, and Peter wrote, and Jude, and all of the rest of the apostles—to help the church in that day and in our day to guard against false teachings.

Now, those apostles writing the New Testament also give us hope, and they tell us about the future, and a lot of other things. But one of their main reasons for writing is to protect us from wrong teaching. For instance, the whole book of Galatians is written against legalism. Legalism started out when the church was born.

So we need somebody to guide us and to help us through this life, so we don't make the wrong choices. We need physical help too. We need somebody to guard us and to lead us.

Jesus tells us in John 10 about the shepherd. He says, "I say unto you, he that entereth not by the door into the sheepfold, but climbeth up some other way, the same is a thief and a robber." He goes on in John 10, and he says, "I am the door." And he says, "I am the good shepherd," and there in verse eleven he says, "The good shepherd giveth his life for the sheep."

In the fourteenth verse, he says again, "I am the good shepherd. I know my sheep, and am known of mine." And he goes on to say how he keeps his sheep, and he protects us, and he holds us in his hand.

Isn't that nice—that I don't have to hang on to Jesus, but Jesus hangs on to me? It's not like I'm hanging over hell, and I'm holding a rope, and I'm hanging on. As long as I can hang onto that rope, I'm not going to go into hell, but if I lose my grip, or I get a little tired and I slip, I can be lost forever. That's not the gospel at all.

In John 10 especially, but in other places in Scripture as well, we're told that God takes us and he holds us in his hands, and we don't have to hold on to anything. We're to rejoice over that, because he says, "I hold them in my hands, and they shall never perish, and nobody will pluck them out of my Father's hand." We're pretty safe, I'd say.

We have this wonderful Shepherd, who goes before us and clears the way, who watches our paths and helps us. He helps us with the decisions of life, and he keeps us safe in life. And if we have an accident, God allows it to teach us something. There's a purpose and a reason for everything that happens in the life of the Christian.

When we love the Lord, it doesn't mean that you're never going to have a car accident. The way some of these people drive, the Lord only knows how he'd ever protect some people. The Lord only knows, but maybe we do have an accident. God doesn't say we'll never be in the hospital, or never stub our toe, because God leads us in different ways. And he uses us in different ways.

Some of our greatest hymns came from people who had terrible suffering. Christian people have lost loved ones, and gone through awful trials, and God has blessed his church for hundreds and hundreds of years because he let some of them go down into that dark valley and suffer. And out of that valley came many hymns.

You can't get perfume without crushing the flowers it comes from. And for God to get perfume from some of us, to become the person he wants us to be, the person he needs for a certain task, there has to be some crushing. So if it needs to be, send it, Lord, because we want your will to be done.

Our Shepherd leads us, and his eyes are ever on us.

We have this wonderful Savior Jesus with us, who says "I am with you always" as our High Priest. I need a priest to intercede for me. I don't need an earthly priest, because they're flesh and blood like I am, but I need a priest in heaven who's at the throne of God. And if you want to have God, you go through his Son Jesus, because he's that priest interceding for us.

The writer of Hebrews put it this way: "Jesus lives forever." He's talking about these other priests after the order of Aaron, who were replaced by the order of Melchizedek. He's talking about earthly priests, and now he says, "But Jesus lives forever, and continues to be a priest, so that no one else is needed."

In the Old Testament they were always getting new priests, because a priest would die, so they had to bring a new one in. And the writer of Hebrews says, "We don't need that anymore, because Jesus never dies." So it all ends up with Jesus Christ as our High Priest. Jesus lives forever, and continues to be our priest, so that no one else is needed.

He is able to save completely all who come to God through him. Since Jesus will live forever, he will always be there as the one who has paid for our sins with his blood. Because Satan accuses us before God;

every time we sin, he's there to accuse us. Now, I don't know how that works, but you read it in the book of Job, where Satan accuses Job before God. We may not fully understand that, but that's Scripture, that's what happens.

When we gossip about somebody, that's a sin. It's a terrible sin. So then Satan says, "Hey, look at Sister So-and-So, look at Brother So-and-So. They're passing around gossip. Look at that one with envy in his eyes. He's envious of his brother, he's jealous." And Satan tells God, "Look there at what a jealous old thing your child is." Or we can be as self-righteous as any Pharisee ever thought of being, as we look down on others, and Satan will bring that to God.

But we have a High Priest, Jesus. He is therefore exactly the kind of high priest we need. For he is holy and blameless, unstained by sin, undefiled by sinners. And to him has been given the place of honor in heaven.

Jesus never needs the daily blood of animal sacrifices to cover our sins. The other priests needed that—first to cover over their own sins, and then to cover the sins of the people. But Jesus finished all sacrifices once and for all when he sacrificed himself on the cross. That's why we don't have sacrifices today. When Jesus sacrificed himself once and for all on the cross, that was the end of sacrifices.

We read in the book of Hebrews that under the old system, even the high priests were weak and sinful men, who couldn't keep from doing wrong. But later God, by his oath, appointed his Son as High Priest, who is perfect forever. That means that we have a priest interceding for us. So he tells us, "I'm always with you. I'll be with you from day one until the day you finish your earthly course, and I call you home." That High Priest is there to love us, and to pray for us, and to support us.

And when Jesus says, "Lo, I am with you always," he says this as your friend. We don't have many friends who are really friends, that you can just open up your heart to. You need to be careful who you're talking to. Don't just open your heart to every person that comes along.

There are very few people you can really trust. Watch out. If you've got one or two, you're very fortunate. But with Jesus we have a friend who never disappoints us, and he never tattles on us. He never lets us down, and he never breaks his word, and he's never tired of us. We can tell our story to him, and it can be ever so poorly told, and it can take forever. You've probably talked to people and asked them how they are, and they start telling you about their ailments all the way down to their ingrown toenails. You ask them how they are, and they give you an organ recital. You wonder if they're ever going to get done.

Or sometimes you're the one who's talking, and as you try to say more and more, pretty soon they're looking off over somewhere, and you know that you might as well be talking to a post. But Jesus is a dependable friend, and he will never tire of us. He understands where we're coming from. He understands and knows all about us. And he's always with us.

The writer of Proverbs says, "There is a friend that sticketh closer than a brother." I have brothers. I have one brother especially, that if I ever got into trouble, I could go to him. He's a friend. Jesus is a friend that sticks even closer than a brother. I also have brothers in the Spirit, and if I had troubles and couldn't pay my bills, I know who I'd go to. I know they would help me out. But there's a friend that sticketh closer than a spiritual brother, and that's the Lord Jesus.

There's an old hymn (by James G. Small) that puts it so well:

I've found a friend, O such a friend!
Christ loved me ere I knew him.
He drew me with the cords of love,
and thus he bound me to him.
And round my heart still closely twine
those ties which naught can sever,
for I am His, and Christ is mine,
forever and forever.
I found a friend, O, such a friend,
so kind and true and tender.
So wise a counselor and guide,
so mighty a defender!
From him who loves me now so well,
what power my soul can sever?
Shall life or death, or earth or hell?
No, I am his forever.

He's my friend. And he's there to help me as I move through this life. As I travel along, there are a lot of times we need a friend. There are a lot of times we need somebody to talk to. Jesus will listen, and he'll be there. We are all in that boat.

I read a story about a young girl in grade school, and her name was Stephanie, and everybody loved Stephanie. She just took the heart of everybody. It wasn't that she was such a beautiful girl. As a matter of fact, she was just very ordinary and plain looking. She wore horn-rimmed glasses, and she was skinny as a bean pole. And yet everybody just loved Stephanie.

They asked her one day, "Stephanie, why is it that everybody loves you?" And she said, "I guess it's because I remember something my grandmother taught me. She said, 'Never forget, Stephie, everybody is a little bit lonesome.'"

Well, I guess that's true. We can be a friend on an earthly level, and we ought to be friends, and we ought to help others and listen to others and be sensitive to their needs. You could be sitting by somebody with a broken heart and never even know it.

Joseph Parker was a great preacher long ago in London. And he said, "Speak to the suffering, and you will never lack an audience. There is a broken heart in every crowd."[22] Could be.

So be an earthly friend, but always remember, you have a friend in Jesus who loves you.

I would like to close by saying that because Jesus is my Lord and my Savior, he also has to be my King. He has to be Lord over me. He has to be the one I give allegiance to. I can't give full allegiance to anything on earth. God has to be first. He asks for that, he calls for that, he deserves that.

Yes, he is with me. He's with me always, he's with me forever. G. Campbell Morgan said it this way:

All our days—days of sunshine and of shadow, days of strength and days of weakness, days of battle and days of victory, the longest day and the shortest day—that one who's with us needs to be our King, needs to be our Lord.

Have we really crowned this King? If we're only interested in him, we sadly fail. On his head are many diadems. He is waiting for the crown of our manhood, our womanhood. He cannot rest in us, until he has our love and our loyalty.

If we reply, "Yes, he is our King"—then where are we obeying him, in his final command, "Go ye therefore, and disciple the nations"?

Are we helping to make our own nation like him? Are we winning a vigil of souls to him? Is the highest passion of our life to weave another garland wherewith to deck his brow, to place another gem in his diadem? If not, then to see such a King and not to obey him is to add to our condemnation. But to see him, and know him, and crown him, and to suffer with him as we serve—that is life indeed.[23]

Everybody can have Jesus if they want. If you don't have him, it's because you've turned him away. But maybe today you will say, "Yes, I need this Jesus. I need his help. I need his understanding. I need his friendship and his fellowship."

Maybe you've already accepted the Lord. You just need to make a stand and let people know: "Yeah, I'm trusting Jesus." Maybe you should rededicate your life or join a church. I am not sure what your next step is, but if the Holy Spirit is talking to your heart, I hope you'll respond, and let the whole world know what decision you're making for Christ.

Lord, we love you today. We thank you, that you are truly a friend. You're our Savior, you're our High Priest, you're our King, you're our Shepherd. You're our everything. Oh, my prayer is that everyone reading this will trust this Jesus, receive him into their heart, and have all these things for their own. We pray in Jesus's name. Amen.

PART IV

The Sacrifice
of Jesus

THE PRECIOUS
BLOOD OF
CHRIST

1 Peter 1:17-25

And if you call on the Father, who without partiality judges according to each one's work, conduct yourselves throughout the time of your stay here in fear; knowing that you were not redeemed with corruptible things, like silver or gold, from your aimless conduct received by tradition from your fathers, but with the precious blood of Christ, as of a lamb without blemish and without spot. He indeed was foreordained before the foundation of the world, but was manifest in these last times for you who through Him believe in God, who raised Him from the dead and gave Him glory, so that your faith and hope are in God.

FROM THESE SCRIPTURES, WE'RE GOING TO FOCUS ON the precious blood of Christ. You don't hear much about the blood of Christ these days. And I'm told that some of the modern hymnals don't even have songs about his blood. And if they do, churches don't use them.

The same thing is true of illustrations. As I prepared this sermon, I got to thinking, I have two books of sermon illustrations, one of 744 pages and another with 650 pages. The first one was published in 1947, the second in 1998. There's a span of fifty years between those two books of illustrations. I looked into those books, and the older one has sixty-three illustrations relating to the blood of Christ. Do you know how many the newer book had? None. They had five illustrations on the cross of Christ, but none on the blood of Christ.

So that tells us something. It tells us that the blood of Jesus Christ is important, and you need not neglect it.

In the devotional resource *Our Daily Bread,* David C. Egner tells of a time when he donated blood. As blood was being drawn from his veins, he was given a card to read that showed the percentages of Americans with different blood types. The two most common are O Positive, with 37.4 percent of the people, and A Positive, with 35.7 percent. The least common blood types are B Negative, with only 1.5 percent, and AB Negative, the rarest blood type, at only 0.6 percent—which is one in every 167 people. Below all these figures on the card was this statement: "The rarest blood type is the one that's not there when you need it."[24]

Well, I'm going to tell you, friend, there's another kind of a blood type. It's the blood of Jesus Christ, and it's something that you need.

You need it because we're told in 1 John 1:7 that the blood of Jesus Christ cleanses us from all sin. The redeemed in heaven are singing right now about that wonderful blood of Christ. In Revelation 1:5, they sing praise "unto him that loved us and washed us from our sins, in his own blood." Praise God for that.

In this chapter, we're going to talk about that wonderful blood of Christ. The apostle Peter says we're redeemed with the precious blood of Christ. That's how important it is.

On a human level, if you lose your blood, you lose your life. And because the blood is what ties our body and our soul together, and our spirit and soul and body. When that blood has gone, life has gone. So blood is extremely important on a human level.

When we come to the Bible, we find that Satan is at war with God. And in order for Jesus Christ to defeat him and to win this battle, he had to shed his blood. That's how important it is. The apostle John describes how the devil wages war against God's people, and John says that they overcame him by the blood of the lamb. That was the way God had a victory over sin—through the blood of the lamb, the blood of Jesus Christ. He had victory over them because Jesus Christ shed his blood on the cross. That was the thing that put Satan down, and it will defeat Satan forever when that time comes.

Clarence Macartney talks about the importance of the blood when he says, "A man may have a perfectly framed and beautiful body, but if drained of its blood, then it becomes nothing but a dead body, a clod."[25]

The Old Testament instilled an awful reverence for blood because it declares, "Whoso sheddeth man's blood, by man shall his blood be shed." For the life of the flesh is in the blood, the Bible teaches; the blood is that which connects and holds the man's body and soul.

If all blood is that precious, how much more precious is the blood of Jesus Christ! When we talk about the blood of Jesus Christ, we're talking about the gospel. We're talking about redemption. We're talking about salvation. We're not just talking about blood that was poured out on the cross, but we're talking about the giving of life, the life of Jesus Christ on the cross, so that he might give unto us everlasting life, if we would take it.

From Genesis to Revelation, the Bible talks about the blood. There's the blood, always the blood. You remember when Moses came down with the law from Mount Sinai and he had that tablet with the law? He sprinkled it with blood. That's a picture of what we see all through the Bible. All through it, you read about the blood. It's a scarlet thread, the crimson ribbon that runs from Genesis to Revelation. There's always that blood. My friend, you have to be as blind as a bat if you're going to miss that. If you don't think about it, and you don't talk about it, and you don't love it, it just means that you won't look at it. So, let's look at that trail of blood through the Bible.

It starts in the book of Genesis. It starts when Adam and Eve sinned against God, and he put judgment on them. And then he clothed them with skins. In order to clothe them with skins, there had to be the shedding of blood. That comes very early in the very first book, in the very first part of the book. There's the shedding of blood. And it goes on all through the book until it comes to the book of Revelation with the scene about the wonderful blood of Christ that cleanses and takes away our sin. When you study that scarlet thread, the crimson ribbon running through the Bible, you'll begin to see the emphasis that God places upon the blood of Jesus Christ. You can't put too much emphasis on it, because God has put the trump card on that wonderful blood that was shed, the blood of his own precious Son.

In Genesis 4, you have the story of Abel's lamb. Abel took a lamb, and he brought it as a sacrifice. He sacrificed it to God, and God accepted it. Undoubtedly, it was slain and then burned. With the death of the lamb, the blood was shed. And it's indicated that it was an offering, because the Bible talks about it. And the fat thereof would burn as a sacrifice that was given to God. And so, this is the first sacrifice in the Bible. It's a sacrifice from Abel, and Abel presented it on behalf of himself.

Well then, you go on to Genesis 22, and we're told that God commanded Abraham, "Take now thy son, thine only son, Isaac, whom thou lovest. Get thee into the land of Moriah and offer him there for a burnt offering." Now, heathens were offering their children to God for sacrifice. So, God is saying, "Abraham, do you love me as much as the heathen?"

Early in the morning, Abraham took his son Isaac. His whole heart is in Isaac, and he takes him to the mount. On that mount, he builds an altar. He puts on the wood, and he binds Isaac, who may have been twenty years old by that time. He wasn't some little boy. He could have resisted, but he didn't. Abraham takes the knife, and he's about to take the life of his son. And lo and behold in the thicket, there's a lamb.

There's a ram that's caught in the thicket. That ram is used for the sacrifice, and Isaac is spared.

You have two things here. You have the blood of the sacrifice, and you have a substitute. Somebody took Isaac's place.

Somebody has also taken your place, and somebody took my place. The picture is beautiful. It's the Lamb of God, Jesus, going to the cross. The Father loves the Son, and yet, the Father is going to take his own Son's life because that blood needs to be shed. There has to be the shedding of blood.

Well then, you come to Exodus 12, and you have the Passover lamb. The children of Israel are slaves in Egypt. They're slaves, and they're under that horrible hand of Egypt. But God is going to liberate them, and he does it by sending a plague through the land.

And God says, "You're to take a lamb, and you're to catch the blood in a basin. And you're to sprinkle it on the doorposts." And when a death angel comes in, the firstborn in every family—both Hebrew and Egyptian—is going to die if there isn't blood. The angel wasn't looking for a good man or a bad man. He was looking for the blood on the doorpost. That's all that was accounted—only the blood. If the blood of the lamb was applied, then that house was safe, and the firstborn was safe. The lamb was slain for a family, and this family was safe because of this wonderful lamb.

Then you go on to the book of Leviticus, and in Leviticus 16, we have the ritual of the two young goats. In the Bible, a young goat is equivalent to a lamb. And the one goat is slain, and then put to death. Then the blood of the slain goat is sprinkled on the living goat, and the living goat is set free to go. And there you have a beautiful picture, because here's a living goat or lamb, and it has all the marks of death. He has the marks of death, but he's alive. It's the picture of Christ dying and raised again.

Jesus Christ has those marks today. He has them on his hands. He has them on his side. He has them on his feet. I think he'll have marks also on his forehead, where they jammed down that thorny crown, sharp as a razor blade, into his head. All those marks are a picture of the death and resurrection of Jesus who died and came to life, and he has the marks of death upon him.

So first we have Abel, and it's a picture of a lamb slain for one person. Then you come to the Passover, and it's a lamb slain for a family. Then you have the ritual of the two goats, and it's a lamb for a nation, for all of Israel. You see what's happening?

Well then, you come to Isaiah 53. And we're told something else about that lamb. We have a new development. We find that the lamb that is slain is going to be a man. This is what it says, in verse 3: "He is despised and rejected of men, a man of sorrows. And yet, we did esteem him stricken, smitten of God and afflicted." And in verse 7: "He was oppressed, and he was afflicted. Yet, he opened not his mouth. He is brought as a lamb to the slaughter, and as a sheep before its shearer is dumb, so he opened not his mouth." Glory to God, the lamb is going to be a man.

Then, look at John 1. Here, you see a prophet whose name is John the Baptist. And God says, "There was a man sent from God, and his name was John." You want to pay attention when a man is sent from God. How powerful that is! And we are told in Luke 1:5 that this man John would be "great in the sight of the Lord, and shall drink neither wine nor strong drink. He shall be filled with the Holy Ghost even from his mother's womb." That's John the Baptist. Listen to what Jesus said about John the Baptist: "Among them that are born of women, there has not risen a greater than John the Baptist" (Matthew 11:11).

Luke tells us about John after his birth: "And the child grew and became strong in spirit, and was in the desert till the day of his showing unto Israel." So John, as soon as he is able, goes out into the desert, and he lives in the desert. He's out in the Judean wilderness. He's dressed with camel's skin, with the skins of animals, and with camel hair that makes up part of his garment. He eats wild honey, and he eats locusts. He lives out there all by himself. And he became a shaggy man from living in the desert, but he's with God. He's not with anybody. He's not at any seminary. He's with God, all alone, this man of God, called of God. He's alone in the desert.

And then this shaggy man comes from the desert, and there's a host of people around in this Jordan Valley along the Jordan River. And to all those multitudes of people, John the Baptist comes. He was a shaggy man, but a fierce man. He points to Jesus Christ and he says, "Behold, the Lamb of God, which takes away the sins of the world." What is he saying? Jesus is that man! Jesus is the Lamb of God that's going to die.

So, there it is. In Genesis 4, the blood of the lamb for the individual. In Exodus 12, the blood of the lamb for a family. In Leviticus 16, the blood of the lamb for a nation. In John 1, the blood of the lamb for the whole world. This is a Savior for the whole world, a message for the whole world.

This is all confirmed later. The Lamb of God is Jesus, and it's confirmed in Acts 8. It's the story of Philip, as he goes into the desert place near Gaza. And here comes the Ethiopian eunuch, and he's riding in his chariot. He's a treasurer for Candace, the queen of the Ethiopians. He was a secretary of the treasury. He's a high official coming from Jerusalem. What has he been doing in Jerusalem? He's been at the temple worshiping. He's not a Jew, but he could come to certain parts of the temple. And he came to worship the God of the Jews.

He's riding in this fancy chariot, with his own horseman driving it. As the chariot moves along, the eunuch is reading out loud—which they did a lot of times; they would read out loud as they traveled. And Philip walks alongside the chariot, and here's the eunuch reading words from Isaiah 53. That was the Scripture which he was reading. The Holy Spirit tells us exactly what the Ethiopian eunuch was reading, and it was these words: "He was led as a sheep to the slaughter, and like a lamb dumb before his shearers, so opened he not his mouth. In his humiliation, his judgment [that is, justice for him] was taken away, and who shall declare this generation? For his life is taken from the earth."

He was denied justice, this Lamb of God. Jesus was denied justice. It says, "Who shall declare his generation?" That is, who in the world is going to express the wickedness of this generation who takes an innocent man and murders him? That's what he's saying. Isaiah is talking about a sheep going to slaughter and also about a man that people are going to crucify. And who is that man? That's what the eunuch was wondering.

So Philip walks by the chariot. And pretty soon, he says, "Do you understand what you're reading?" The Ethiopian says, "No. How can I understand it, unless somebody explains it?"

So Philip joined with the man, and he preached Jesus unto him. He was saying, that man Isaiah speaks of is Jesus Christ. There can be no question about it.

And then we come to Revelation. What do you get in Revelation? Well, we don't sing about it here, but this is what they sing about in heaven: "Unto him that hath loved us and washed it with our sin, and washed us from our sins in his own blood, and hath made us kings and priests unto God and his Father, to him be glory and dominion forever and ever, amen." So the crimson cord of blood continues into the book of Revelation, where they're singing the praises of God. And we have a lot of loved ones singing over there right now.

We are going to be there too. We're going to sing about the precious blood of Jesus Christ. And rightly so, because don't you see? Look at this. By the power of the Lord Jesus Christ, his blood justifies us. It's the blood that justifies us. As Paul declared in Romans 5:9, we're "being now justified by his blood."

That justification simply means that you and I are sinners, because we've all committed some sin, and before God we can't get into heaven, because God is holy and just. We are unjust, and we are sinners, and we can't get into heaven. We sinned against God. We broke his law. But Jesus took our place on the cross, and he shed his blood. And he paid for our sins. And he justifies the poor lost sinner.

When I get to heaven, I'll be just like Jesus Christ, because I'm clothed in his righteousness. And the moment you accept Jesus Christ, you're perfectly clothed in his righteousness. In fact you'll never be any more righteous than on the day you accept Jesus.

I accepted Jesus when I was ten years old. That's almost ninety years ago. I'm not any more justified now than I was as a poor little kid out on the farm, a scrawny little thing who didn't know up from down. But I knew enough to ask and call on the name of the Lord, and I was justified. And I was justified as much then as I am now.

You're made perfect in Christ—that's the power of the blood.

The blood also redeems us. Jesus Christ has a lot of names in the Bible: Lord, Savior, King, Priest, Mediator, Mighty God, Prince of Peace. And probably the best of all is Redeemer. He has redeemed us.

As Job said a long time ago, "I know that my Redeemer liveth." We can know that too, because of that blood shed for us.

I have a Savior, and I'm going to be raised again, and I'll see the Lord—"whom I shall see for myself, and mine eyes shall behold, and not another" (Job 19:27). I'm going to see God face to face, all because of Jesus.

Job didn't know anything about Jesus, but he knew about a kinsman redeemer. We're a part of a kinsman who would die for somebody else. So Jesus became one of us, and he died for us. And Job is clothed with that righteousness, just like we are. He's redeemed.

In Paul's day, half of the world was in slavery. People bought slaves, and they sold them. We sing about how we are all poor lost sinners, and in fact we're slaves to sin. But Jesus paid the price to redeem us from that slavery. And so we sing the old hymn, "Jesus paid it all, all to him I owe. Sin had left a crimson stain. He washed it white as snow." The blood of Jesus Christ saves us, takes us, and redeems us.

The blood of Jesus Christ reconciles us. In Isaiah 59:2 we read, "Your iniquities have separated between you and your God." Isaiah is talking here to the people of Israel. "Your iniquities have separated between you and your God, and your sins have hid his face from you, so that he will not hear."

That's what sin always does. Sin always separates. It separates friends. Have you ever had a friend, and because of sin and misunderstanding, you were separated? Couples are separated because of sin. Married couples are separated because of sin. Sin separates us from God, not from just each other, but from God.

We read about Cain, how he went out from the presence of the Lord after he committed murder. We read about Judas, who betrayed Jesus, and then he went out. And the Bible says, "And it was night." And what a dark black night that was, when Peter denied Jesus! And he went out and wept bitterly.

Can humanity be made right with God? Can humanity be reconciled to God? Yes, by the precious blood of Jesus. He brings us back into fellowship with him. We were enemies of God, but Paul tells us in Romans that when we were enemies of God, Jesus went to the cross and he died for his enemies.

We were reconciled to God by the blood of his Son, and we're brought back in fellowship. So now, we can talk to God. In Hebrews 13:5, we read how that wonderful Jesus will always be with us. So we don't fear any man, because we have fellowship with the Father. Wonderful, wonderful Jesus!

Then, a fourth thing his blood does, is that it cleanses us. Just think of the soul. It was created in the very image of God, and it was created beautiful and immortal. It was just a perfect creation of God.

But it was stained by sin, and that beautiful, immortal soul became stained and unfit for the presence of God. And there wasn't any way God could receive that into heaven. So we sing the song, "Sin had left the crimson stain." As Isaiah declared, "Though your sins be as scarlet, though they be red like crimson"—you see, that's what happened to that soul. But the blood of Jesus makes us white as snow.

When Adam and Eve sinned in the garden of Eden, that sin passed on to all of us. Now, don't go blaming poor Adam. I'm going to tell you a little secret. If we would have been in the garden of Eden, we would have done the same thing. And even if he didn't sin, have you any sins of your own? Of course, you have. And so, all our beautiful souls are stained.

Then we come to this wonderful scripture telling us that the blood of Jesus Christ will take away all that sin, will wash all that sin away. "The blood of Jesus Christ cleanses us from all of our sin" (1 John 1:7).

There are many people with a stained soul and a stained spirit. There are many people who haven't come under the blood of Christ. And why is it that they don't come? We have a personal invitation from Jesus. You can come to the Lord Jesus, and you can find everlasting life. And so, you need to look to the Lord. Trust in the Lord.

I read the story of an officer killed in battle in the middle of the Civil War, and his body was taken home to his widowed mother in Alabama. His mother stood waiting for him on the doorstep as they carried up his body. And through her tears, she whispered, "Washed in the blood of the lamb that was slain." That's the only thing that counts.

I don't care who you are, or what you are, or what you think you are, you have nothing when you come to the end of the road except the blood of Jesus Christ. Are you washed in the blood of the lamb that was slain?

You say, "Well, how can I do that?" That's what Nicodemus asked Jesus. He said, "How can I be born again?" He didn't understand it. And Jesus answered Nicodemus, and he's answering you, and this is his answer (in John 3:18): "He that believeth on him"—on Jesus— "is not condemned, but he that believeth not is condemned already, because he has not believed in the name of the only begotten Son of God."

That's the answer. Believe on the Son of God. Believe on the Lord Jesus Christ, and you will be washed of your sins. Have you ever prayed that prayer and asked Jesus to come into your heart and take away your sin? You've got to do that, dear friend. You don't have any hope in this world or in the world to come without that precious blood of Jesus Christ.

Now, I'm going to tell you what may be happening with you while you're reading this today. The devil is saying, "Well, you don't need to do it now. Go to some church and do it." Or, "Do it on your birthday. Accept Jesus on your birthday." Wouldn't that be nice? Or, "Wait till Christmas, when Jesus was born in Bethlehem, so he can be born in your heart. Just put it off."

You see, the devil never says, "Don't accept Jesus." He never says that. He's not stupid. He just says, "Put it off. Put it off. Wait. Wait." And I'm going to tell you, dear friend, you can wait, and you can wait, and you can wait. But one of these days will be your last. And I don't know when, and you don't know when. But it's going to come. And the scripture says that after death, the judgment. After death, there's no changing. You're in heaven or you're in hell. You're under the blood, or you're not under the blood. That's all.

It isn't difficult. I was ten years old, and I understood it. You can understand it if you want to. So, I'm praying that you will ask Jesus to come into your heart.

Dear heavenly Father, we're just so thankful that we can be a part of the body of Christ. And we don't even know how big that is. We don't know how many there are, but we know that we're all a part of your body, and you are the head. And we're members of that body. And so, we just pray that you'll help us to love you and to trust you. We pray that all we can do and say will be an honor to your name. We pray, Lord, that the devil would be rebuked by the blood of Jesus Christ that we've openly spoken of, and we'll find in that blood the remission of sins, and eternal life, everlasting life. And then, with that everlasting life, we find fellowship with the Lord Jesus. And that wonderful fellowship with us, in the night when we can't sleep, is with us wherever we go. We have that wonderful fellowship with your dear Son. So, we thank you for Jesus. We pray it all in his wonderful name, amen.

CHRIST IS RISEN—
NOW WHAT?

Matthew
26:31-34, 26:69-75

Then Jesus said to them, "All of you will be made to stumble because of Me this night, for it is written: 'I will strike the Shepherd, and the sheep of the flock will be scattered.' But after I have been raised, I will go before you to Galilee."

Peter answered and said to Him, "Even if all are made to stumble because of You, I will never be made to stumble."

Jesus said to him, "Assuredly, I say to you that this night, before the rooster crows, you will deny Me three times."

...Now Peter sat outside in the courtyard. And a servant girl came to him, saying, "You also were with Jesus of Galilee."

But he denied it before them all, saying, "I do not know what you are saying."

And when he had gone out to the gateway, another girl saw him and said to those who were there, "This fellow also was with Jesus of Nazareth."

But again he denied with an oath, "I do not know the Man!"

And a little later those who stood by came up and said to Peter, "Surely you also are one of them, for your speech betrays you."

Then he began to curse and swear, saying, "I do not know the Man!" Immediately a rooster crowed. And Peter remembered the word of Jesus who had said to him, "Before the rooster crows, you will deny Me three times." So he went out and wept bitterly.

Now I want us to think about the resurrection of Jesus Christ. And we have the story of Peter, and how he had failed. Yet through the work of our Lord, that man was saved and he was kept and he was restored. And we can be kept also by the great power of this wonderful God. On Easter Sunday we celebrate when the women went to the tomb, and the angel said to them, "He is not here. He is risen, as he said. Come, see the place where the Lord lay."

The resurrection of Jesus Christ is a solid, definite, historical fact. It isn't a theory. It isn't some kind of a dream. The New Testament testifies that the body of Jesus was taken down from the cross and placed in a tomb that belonged to Joseph of Arimathea. And history declares that on the following Sunday morning, the tomb was empty.

Everyone admits this, that this tomb was empty that first Easter Sunday morning. Whether you're a Christian or an unbeliever, a disciple or a scoffer, a Jew or a Gentile, whether you're conservative or moderate or liberal or whatever you are, you have to admit the truth, because it's historical fact that on the first Easter Sunday morning, the tomb was empty.

Now, of course, there are those who try to make up reasons for how it was empty, but there isn't any reasonable way to explain the empty tomb except to say that Christ is risen.

I want to say again, when we talk about the resurrection of Christ, don't let somebody pooh-pooh you and say, "Well, that's in the Bible, but

243

the Bible isn't all true, and I don't believe the Bible anyway." Because the reality of the resurrection of Jesus Christ is something we judge as we do any other historical event. The criteria for determining how Caesar waged war against Gaul, or how the Goths sacked Rome, or what happened at Waterloo, are the same criteria by which we determine what happened on that first Easter Sunday morning. So you don't have to take a back seat to anyone.

Jesus Christ is risen from the grave, and that grave was empty. People try to explain it in different ways. You can look at all the theories, but they don't stand up under any kind of scrutiny. So you can be happy that we know of the risen Christ.

Jesus Christ appeared on at least ten different occasions after his resurrection. For instance, he appeared to certain women as they returned from the sepulchre after having seen the angel who told them that Christ had risen. He appeared to Mary Magdalene at the sepulchre, probably upon her second visit to it that morning.

He appeared to the apostle Peter before the evening of the day of the resurrection, but under circumstances of which we have no details. He appeared also to two disciples, Cleopas and another, who were on the way to Emmaus on the afternoon of that day. He appeared to the ten apostles—Thomas being absent—together with others whose names are not given, all assembled together for the evening meal of that day.

One week later, he appeared to all the eleven apostles, and he appeared probably in the same place as the preceding appearance. Later he appeared to several of the disciples at the Sea of Galilee while they were fishing, though the exact time is undesignated.

He also appeared to more than five hundred brethren at once on an appointed mountain in Galilee. He appeared to James under circumstances of which we have no information. And then he appeared to the apostles outside Jerusalem immediately before his ascension on the Mount of Olives.

There can be no question that Jesus Christ's resurrection is a historical fact, and it has been witnessed by at least ten different groups of people, one of them being five hundred people at once. The resurrection is an established fact, and we rejoice in it. Don't be afraid to talk about the resurrection. Don't be afraid to let people know where you stand on the resurrection, because all through the centuries, beginning with the first century, there have been those who've stood firm for the resurrection of Jesus Christ.

For instance, the greatest man in the first century of the Christian era was the apostle Paul. He always testified of Christ's resurrection from the grave. The greatest man in the fourth century was Saint Augustine. He never wearied of talking about the resurrection of our Lord. The man who is recognized as probably the greatest intellect of modern times, Sir Isaac Newton, also believed in the resurrection of Jesus Christ.

Do you realize that most of the famous universities in the United States were founded and were first led by men who believed in the resurrection of Jesus Christ? For instance, Increase Mather was president of Harvard, and his writings and teachings talked about the resurrection of Jesus Christ. And there was Timothy Dwight, president of Yale, and Nathan Lord, president of Dartmouth, and Edward Hitchcock, president of Amherst; and Mark Hopkins, president of Williams College, and John Witherspoon, president of Princeton, and on and on. These all believed in a literal physical resurrection of Jesus Christ.

I'm going to leave it at that. I could write a whole book on that. But because we have a resurrected Christ, we have some wonderful truths to draw upon, and I want to mention some of them quickly.

Because of the resurrection of Jesus Christ, we have a Savior. Sometimes people don't worry too much about a savior until they come to die. But somewhere along the line, there's a reckoning time. And if they have any time to think before their death, things look a lot different. They think about their past, and they think about the judgment to come.

God has instilled in all our hearts a belief in the hereafter, just like a bird has an instinct to fly south in the fall. Sometimes birds fly way out into the middle of the Pacific Ocean to a little island, and even young birds that have never been there before have that instinct. And we have that instinct about what comes after death, that there's got to be something beyond this life. There's got to be a hereafter. There's a heaven and there's a hell, and there's a judgment to come. And when we're honest and sober, we have to admit this, because God has placed it in every heart and soul. These things are real. And when we have Jesus Christ, we have a living Savior.

Abraham is the founder of the Jewish nation, of the Jewish people. But Abraham died and is buried in Hebron. They've built a mosque over the burial place of Abraham and Sarah and others. He's dead. The founder of the Jewish nation is dead.

Or you can take Buddha, for instance. His followers never ascribe a resurrection to Buddha. They don't even dream of such a thing.

Or take Muhammad, the founder of the Muslim faith, who died on June 8, in the year 632, at the age of sixty-one. He died at Medina, and there he is buried.

So when it comes to all of these people, the millions and millions of Buddhists and Jews and Muslims, none of them claim that they have a risen founder or a risen savior. But we, as believers in Christ, have that, and we ought to rejoice in it. And because we have a risen Christ, we have a Savior from our sin.

Second, we now have justification, because we have the risen Jesus Christ. Paul says in Romans 4:25 that Jesus "was delivered for our offenses, and was raised again for our justification." It simply means this: Jesus died for our sins, but how do we know that his death was acceptable to God for that purpose? How do we know that God accepted the death of Jesus Christ on the cross to pay for the sins of the whole world?

We didn't know, for as long as he was in the tomb for those three days. We didn't know if God accepted that as full payment or not. But when Jesus Christ was raised from the dead, he showed, "It is paid in full." He has more than paid for your sins, and it's all taken care of. It's all settled.

That's a great thought to have, especially when you get a little older and you know that you're going to come to death one of these days. Just to know that all my sins are gone, all gone because of Jesus's blood on the cross. All my past and present sins are gone, and all the future sins that I'll commit before I die—they're all covered under the blood. They're all taken away. I'm justified in the sight of God.

Some people can't understand how God can forgive our sins in the future. But dear friend, all of our sins were in the future when Jesus died, because we had not yet even been born. They're all paid, and when we receive Jesus Christ, we are justified in his sight.

Third, we have hope. When a person loses hope, they lose life. When they lose hope, they lose the willingness to go on, to move on. You have to have dreams, and you have to have hope, and you have to have challenges in order to go on and to move on. We have that in Jesus. He is that wonderful hope. He is our blessed hope.

When Peter thought that Jesus was dead, his hope was gone. And what did Peter say? He said, "I'm going fishing." He meant that he was going to Galilee, and he was going back to an old kind of life, the life he used to have as a professional fisherman.

A few years earlier, when Jesus came and told him to leave the nets, he left those nets, and he left his home, and he left his parents, and he went with Jesus. Jesus was his hope. And he believed that Jesus was the Messiah who would set up a kingdom, and he was going to rule it all. But when Jesus died, it dashed Peter's hopes, and he had no other reason to live. So he said, "I'm going back to my old way of life. I'm going back to fishing."

But when he saw the risen Christ, he didn't have time for fishing anymore. And when Christ forgave him for his sins, Peter took heart, and he lived for Christ the rest of his life. And when the time came for Peter to die, tradition says that he was crucified, but he asked to be crucified head-down, because he wasn't worthy to die in the same way as his Lord.

Hope took Peter through all of those things. Peter writes in his first epistle, "Blessed be the God and Father of our Lord Jesus Christ, who according to his abundant mercy hath begotten us again unto a living hope by the resurrection of Jesus Christ from the dead, to an inheritance incorruptible and undefiled, and that fadeth not away, reserved in heaven for you who are kept by the power of God through faith unto salvation, ready to be revealed at the last time." Because of the resurrection, we have hope.

Then fourth, we're told that the resurrected Jesus Christ holds us and keeps us. We don't have to walk with fear, wondering if we're going to be lost at last, because he says, "I'll keep you." We sing the song, "I Know Whom I Have Believed," and we declare that we know the Lord will keep that which we have committed unto him against that day. He's going to take all of my sins, and I'm never going to see them again. In her book *Tramp for the Lord*, Corrie ten Boom speaks of how, when we confess our sins, God casts those sins into the deepest ocean, gone forever. And God then places a sign there that says "No Fishing Allowed."

Have you ever thought about sins from your past, some of your failures of the past? I have. And that's the devil's trick, because you can't change the past. There are two things you can't change. You can't change the past, and you can't change the future. All you can change is the present. You have that to handle and to work with.

So when we get to thinking about our past failures, it can drive us crazy. And the devil likes to get you onto that tune, because then he can just drive you crazy. But when you realize that it's all paid for, that it's all settled, that it's all gone—our past, present, and future sins—then we have this wonderful preservation in Jesus Christ.

Jesus said, "My sheep hear my voice. I know them. They follow me. I give unto them eternal life. They shall never perish, neither shall any man pluck them out of my hand. My Father, who gave them to me, is greater than all; and no man is able to pluck them out of my Father's hand."

The Living Bible paraphrases it this way: "My sheep recognize my voice, and I know them, and they follow me. I give them eternal life, and they shall never perish. No one shall snatch them away from me, for my Father has given them to me, and he is more powerful than anyone else. So no one can kidnap them from me."

The writer of Hebrews says about Christ as our High Priest: "Wherefore he is able also to save them to the uttermost that come unto God by him, seeing he ever liveth to make intercession for them." Our wonderful Lord saves them unto the uttermost, the uttermost of sin. That is, you can't sin so much that God won't forgive you.

I talked to a man not very long ago from out of town, a good number of miles away. I was asked to talk to him, so I called him, and he said, "I just don't think God can forgive me for all my sins. I've got some terrible sins." And I gave him this verse, that God will save us to the uttermost of sin. And remember how Paul says that he was "the chief of sinners"—and if God saved the chief of sinners, he can save us.

But really what this scripture in Hebrews is saying is not the uttermost of sin, but for the uttermost of time. He's able to save unto the uttermost, he will save us until we meet Christ in heaven, until we're safe at home. What a wonderful, wonderful Lord! Paul says, "Who is he that condemneth? It is Christ that died, yea rather, that is risen again, who is even at the right hand of God, who also maketh intercession for us." He is the risen Christ. He gives us power and help.

Fifth, we're told that the risen Christ gives us power to live the Christian life. How many times do people say, "Well, I'm not going to start the Christian life because I can't live up to it? I don't want to be a hypocrite, and I know if I start out, then I'll fail. So I'm not going to try, because people will call me a hypocrite." See, that's just the devil giving you a bad time, because nobody is perfect, and nobody can live the Christian life perfectly. We all want to, we all strive for it, and it's our dream and our desire. But none of us make it in this life.

We can work just as hard as we want and strive as hard as we want, but we're never going to be perfect. That's why we're to stop looking at other people. Stop picking that little thing out of their eye when you've got a big log in your own eye. We check, and we see that this one isn't right, and this one isn't right, and this one isn't right. We're doing all this picking around, and what we're doing is picking at the body of Christ. Leave them alone, and live your own life. Let a man examine himself, and keep himself honest.

We have power to live the Christian life. What you have to do is just start out. Don't get cleaned up before you come to Christ. That's the worst thing you can try, because you can't clean up your old nature.

It's just like if you lived with the pioneers. They used to have sod houses that had a dirt floor. If they were going to have company, they might want to clean up the floor. What if they got a bucket of water and soap, and started to mop the mud floors? The more you mop, the worse it gets. You would have a hopeless mess on your hands.

That's what the old nature is. You try to fix up the old nature, and the more you work on it, the bigger mess it's going to be. So you come to Christ, and you ask Christ to save you. He gives us a new nature, and he'll help us clean up our act. God is going to convict us about some things we're doing, or some things we're not doing that we ought to be doing. So just keep in tune with the Lord.

Because we have a risen Christ, we have power. We also have a resurrection. We have many services out in the cemetery, and we'll leave that body out in the cemetery. We will always say, "Jesus Christ has promised that he's coming again, and he'll raise these bodies from the grave. And what he has promised, he'll perform. So the Lord himself shall descend from heaven with a shout, with the voice of the archangel, with the trumpet of God. And the dead in Christ"—that's all the believers who have passed on— "shall rise first. Then we which are alive will be caught up together with them to meet the Lord in the air."

Every Christian friend you have out in the cemetery is going to be raised from the grave. What a great and wonderful day!

But this brings us responsibilities. Because we have a resurrected Christ, we have responsibilities. Peter preaches, and he tells us that we need to be witnesses. On the day of Pentecost, he declared openly, "This Jesus hath God raised up, whereof we are all witnesses." We're all witnesses.

I type out my sermons, and I use an old typewriter. When I type, I make a mistake once in a while—that is, about every other word. When I typed out this word "witness," I typed a typographical error, and I had "sitnesses." I said, "Hey, wait a minute. Maybe that's the Holy Ghost." Because we've got too many "sitnesses" and not enough witnesses. We're sitting.

Not everybody can be a preacher, but everybody can be a witness. You can tell your friends in school, or wherever you work, or wherever you go—tell them what Jesus Christ means to you. Encourage them to come to church or bring them to church, so they hear the preaching of the gospel. We are all witnesses.

The Lord tells us that as long as we live, he's going to call us to be accountable. We can have such a great joy telling other people. Because

Jesus Christ is the most wonderful person in all the world. You never have to be ashamed of Jesus.

It doesn't matter what your background is. It doesn't matter where you come from. Jesus will always fit into that picture. That's the beauty of Jesus. He came so that the whole world would know him. And he fits into every picture, in every way. That's because he's the universal Christ, and he answers every person. He comes into your world, wherever you might be.

An unknown author put it like this,

To the artist, he is the one altogether lovely. To the architect, He is the chief cornerstone. To the baker, he's the living bread. To the banker, he's the hidden treasure. To the biologist, he is the life. To the builder, he is the sure foundation. To the carpenter, he is the door. To the doctor, he is the great physician. To the educator, he is the great teacher. To the engineer, he is the new and living way. To the florist, he is the rose of Sharon and the lily of the valley. To the geologist, he is the rock of ages. To the horticulturist, he is the true vine. To the judge, he is the righteous judge, the judge of all men. To the jeweler, he's the pearl of great price. To the lawyer, he's the counselor, the lawgiver, the advocate.

To the journalist, he's the good news of great joy. To the ophthalmologist, he is the light of the eyes. To the philanthropist, he is the unspeakable gift. To the philosopher, he is the wisdom of God. To the preacher, he is the word of God. To the sculptor, he is the living stone. To the servant, he is the good master. To the statesman, he's the desire of all nations. To the student, he is the incarnate truth. To the theologian, he is the author and finisher of our faith. To the toiler, he is the giver of rest. To the sinner, he is the Lamb of God that taketh away the sins of the world. To the Christian, he is the Son of the living God, the Savior, the Redeemer, the Lord.

That's Jesus Christ, the risen Christ. And every one of us can have a personal relationship with him. We can know him. We can have him with us wherever we go. We can talk to him. We can feel his presence. The longer we walk with the Lord, the more certain we feel our spirit bearing witness with the Holy Spirit, and the Holy Spirit bearing witness with our spirit, that we are the children of God.

I don't put a lot of emphasis on feelings, because you can feel good and you can feel bad, but there does come a time of joy that you just know that you belong to Jesus, and he belongs to you, and everything is just all right.

Thank you for Jesus, dear heavenly Father. Thank you that he loves every one of us. Thank you that he'll never turn anybody away. "Him that cometh unto me, I will no wise cast out." Give help to anyone reading this in praying the prayer of the penitent: "God be merciful to me, a sinner. Save me for Christ's sake, and come into my life." We thank you again that we can walk with you day by day. In Jesus's name, Amen.

IS HE REALLY YOUR LORD?

Acts 10:9-22

The next day, as they went on their journey and drew near the city, Peter went up on the housetop to pray, about the sixth hour. Then he became very hungry and wanted to eat; but while they made ready, he fell into a trance and saw heaven opened and an object like a great sheet bound at the four corners, descending to him and let down to the earth. In it were all kinds of four-footed animals of the earth, wild beasts, creeping things, and birds of the air. And a voice came to him, "Rise, Peter; kill and eat."

But Peter said, "Not so, Lord! For I have never eaten anything common or unclean."

And a voice spoke to him again the second time, "What God has cleansed you must not call common." This was done three times. And the object was taken up into heaven again.

Now while Peter wondered within himself what this vision which he had seen meant, behold, the men who had been sent from Cornelius had made inquiry for Simon's house, and stood before the gate. And they called and asked whether Simon, whose surname was Peter, was lodging there.

While Peter thought about the vision, the Spirit said to him, "Behold, three men are seeking you. Arise therefore, go down and go with them, doubting nothing; for I have sent them."

Then Peter went down to the men who had been sent to him from Cornelius, and said, "Yes, I am he whom you seek. For what reason have you come?"

And they said, "Cornelius the centurion, a just man, one who fears God and has a good reputation among all the nation of the Jews, was divinely instructed by a holy angel to summon you to his house, and to hear words from you."

LET ME START BY SAYING THAT SOME HAVE INTERPRET- ed this passage of Scripture by praying that they'll have the Holy Spirit. Don't do that. You might as well just pray that you have a head on your shoulders, which you already have. When you receive Jesus Christ, you receive the Holy Spirit. That is settled. You don't need to pray an extra prayer to receive the Holy Spirit.

Now, to be *filled* with the Holy Spirit is another matter, because that happens when we submit entirely to the leading of the Holy Spirit. But as far as the *indwelling* of the Holy Spirit is concerned, that happens the moment you accept Jesus Christ. The Holy Spirit is here to help us.

So the Holy Spirit comes to Peter, and Peter goes out and he begins preaching and teaching and working for the Lord. At first, he does it exclusively with the Jews, because that's the way he'd been raised. He shares with them the good news of Jesus Christ who was crucified and raised again. He shares the good news with the Jews alone. He tells them that Jesus Christ has died for them, but he doesn't go to the Gentiles, and has nothing to do with the Gentiles. As far as he's concerned, they're unredeemable, and he's just not going to even preach to the Gentiles.

But God has given his Son for the Jew and the Gentile both. So he has to go to Peter, and he has to talk to him, because he's going to have the gospel carried to the Gentiles as well as the Jews. But Peter doesn't know that, because all through the Old Testament, the special favor of

God was on the Jew. And in Scripture it says, "We preach to the Jew first and then to the Gentile." So it was always to the Jews, and that's all that Peter could understand.

He had some very deep-seated prejudices against the Gentiles, and there was no place in his program for them. What Peter didn't know is that it was at this very point in time God would inspire a ministry outreach to the Gentiles, and Peter was going to be the messenger. He was going to be the preacher who would go to Caesarea and preach to the Gentiles. He never dreamed of such a thing. It never occurred to him.

You may know the story. While Peter was at Joppa, just south of Caesarea, he goes onto the roof of his house. In Palestine, they have those flat roofs; my relatives in Lebanon all have a flat-top house. I've seen them up there in the summer. They take figs and they break the figs open and lay them on those house tops to let them dry. Then they put them all together, and take them and keep them in the winter, and eat those dried figs in the winter time.

It's a flat top, and so Peter is up on this housetop just looking out over the countryside, and he's praying. And while he's praying, he has a vision. In this vision, he sees a sheet lowered from heaven, and on it is every type of animal that God has created. Peter was taught from the Old Testament that there were clean animals and then there were unclean animals that he wouldn't touch. Peter wouldn't dream of touching the unclean animals and birds and reptiles. And in this vision the Lord tells Peter, "Rise and eat." Peter is absolutely astounded at such a thing, because he sees the unclean animals there. So he says to Jesus, "Not so, Lord. No Lord, I'm not going to eat." He's calling him "Lord," but he's telling him no—and that doesn't make sense. We want to be sure we don't do that.

So God tells Peter, "What God has cleansed, you must not call common." In other words, he's saying to Peter, "Don't talk back to me. If I tell you to rise and eat, and if you're my servant, then it's best for you to get up and rise and eat. And Peter, I'm not giving you advice, I'm telling you what to do. I want you to eat of these animals—even the unclean." But Peter has a problem with that.

We may need to be very careful that when God speaks to our heart and calls upon us to stop doing certain things or to start doing things, that we don't say, "No, Lord," or, "No, God, I'm not going to do that." When we postpone, or when we argue, or when we're half-hearted, or when we prolong service, or refuse, or maybe don't give services as quickly as we should, we're saying no to the Lord.

So let's look at that for a few minutes. I want to ask three questions related to saying no to the Lord, as Peter did.

First, what's really so wrong with saying "Not so, Lord," or, "No, Lord?" Well, for one thing it's a total contradiction, a total and complete contradiction. Those two words— "No, Lord"—never belong together. You see, whoever calls himself a Christian and says, "Lord," should never say no to him.

Now, if Jesus Christ isn't your Lord, you can say anything you want. But if he's our Lord and our Master, we can never tell him no.

There are some who say that Jesus can never be your Savior unless he's also your Lord. But that's not so, because there are many people who have Jesus as their Savior, and they don't have him as their Lord. I lived like that at a time in my life too. I was saved, because God's Word says that whosoever will call upon the name of the Lord will be saved, and I called on his name, and I was saved. But he wasn't my Lord.

And I'm not the only one. If you read in 1 Corinthians, you'll see beyond the shadow of a doubt that there were people who were saved, and Jesus Christ was their Savior, but he wasn't their Lord. Paul says that they're saints. He says, "They're saved, they're saints—and yet they're living in sin." And they were so bad that God even had to take some of them out of this world. He says, "Because of your sin, some are sickly among you, and some even sleep."

But we want to be sure that we have Jesus as our Savior but also as our Lord. Like one man said, "I have Jesus, but does Jesus have me? I have him as my Savior, but does he have me as my Lord?" It's a contradiction of terms when we say, "No, Lord."

The second question I want to ask is this: What does it mean then to say "Lord"? What does it mean to say "Lord" and really mean it? How can we tell if he *is* our Lord?

Well, for one thing, to call him Lord and really mean it means that we will embrace his will unconditionally. No questions asked, no strings attached, no small print. We're giving God a blank check, and that check is our life. And we're saying, "I will be your servant. You will be my Lord, and I don't care where it leads or what you ask." Then he becomes our Lord, and that means that we're going to pray like Jesus taught us to pray and like Jesus prayed: "Not my will but thine be done."

And in Jesus's case, doing his Father's will meant going to the cross and dying for the sins of the world. He gave himself on a cross because he was unconditionally giving himself to the Lord God his Father.

So we just want to be sure that we give Christ the first place in our life, before anything else. No love supersedes the love we have for Jesus Christ if we really mean it. And give Peter the credit, he really meant it.

He changed course, as hard as it was. He'd been raised as a stubborn Jew, but when he met his Lord, he went.

To say "Lord" means not only to embrace his will unconditionally, but also to submit to his word specifically. These two statements both go together. That is, when the Lord tells us something, we have to obey it and obey his word.

For instance, let me give you a couple of illustrations. He tells us in his word, "Come out from among them and be separate and touch not the unclean thing." So God is calling for a separated life of his people, and that makes us different. He says that we're the light in the world, and the world is in darkness, and we are a light, and that light in the world is different. He says also that we're the salt of the earth, and if we're salt, we're different than the corruption in the world about us. I wonder where the world would be today if it wasn't for the church of Jesus Christ serving as salt to counteract corruption in the world. You think it's bad now! If the church was taken out—and it will be someday—the corruption will be overwhelming. Thank God for the church.

So the Lord wants us to be separate. He tells us to abstain from all appearance of evil. He doesn't say that the thing might be wrong; he says that if it even looks wrong, don't do it.

He says, for example, "Forsake not the assembling of yourselves together." You ought to be in church. Forsake not the assembling of yourselves together.

Sometimes people get mad at me for saying those things. I remember one time I was preaching on radio, and one of the fellows in our church was up north goose hunting, and listening to the service on the radio. And I said that morning, "If any of you men are out goose hunting, and you ought to be in church, I hope you don't get a shot." And he didn't get a shot that day, and he got mad. He didn't quit the church (half the time they quit the church when they get mad), because he was more of a man than that, and he stood with us.

Since the Scripture tells us we're not to forsake the assembling of ourselves together, if you can get to church you ought to be in church, and you ought to support your church.

So some of these that God gives us to do are very plain, and we need to listen. We just have to look to him, and God says that if he's really Lord, you'll rest in his love. And we just trust Jesus, and we'll go on and we'll serve him to the best of our ability.

But then there's another question I want to ask, my third and final question: Why? Why is it that we would ever say no to the Lord? Why would we even consider such a thing?

I think there are three reasons. One reason is that we may not really understand as much about God as we should. We have an inadequate knowledge of God, and that's what Peter's trouble was. He said no to God, and it wasn't rebellion. Really, it didn't come out of rebellion, but it came out of prejudice. He was taught not to eat those unclean animals, and when God tells him to eat them, he's rebelling in a way, but it's because he has a certain prejudice against these things, and that's the way he's been taught. And he has to get over that.

So much of the time, our prejudice is really a mark of ignorance. We have all kinds of prejudice among us, and as Christian people we have to be very careful of that.

So look at the account, it's very simple. Peter is up on the housetop, and some of these messengers come, and they said, "We would like to see Peter." And the servant of the house says, "Peter's up on the housetop and he's praying, and he's busy, and he won't be able to see you." And they said, "Well, we'd really like to see Peter." So the servant goes to Peter and he says, "There are three men out here who would like to talk to you." And Peter says, "Well, I wonder what they want to see me about? Yeah, I'll see them."

He goes down there to these three. Now listen, Peter has just had this vision where God says, "Don't you call anything unclean, none of these animals unclean, none."

He comes down from the housetop to hear them say, "Our master at Caesarea wants you to come to his home and conduct a series of meetings for us."

"Well, that's fine," Peter says. "Who is your master? Who sent you?"

And they say, "His name is Cornelius, sir. He's the Roman centurion in charge of the garrison at Caesarea."

And right that minute the light comes on in Peter's head. This man who's inviting him is a Roman, he's an uncircumcised Gentile. And Peter had never preached to a Gentile. Gentiles to him were unclean and unfit, and they couldn't even be redeemed.

Then there rings this vision in his heart and his mind. God has said, "What I have cleansed call not thou unclean. Don't you call them common, don't you call them unclean." Peter has just come from that trance. And God has told him—and friend, I'm going to tell you—we need to give a lot of credit to Peter, because he didn't argue with God anymore. He knew what the vision meant. It meant that all people and all creation were worthy of the gospel. And Peter says, "I don't understand, but I see that I'm wrong, because God has talked to me, and I'm going to go to that man's house." And he went to Cornelius, and Cornelius the Gentile was saved.

We have to live in a very careful way. We have to be sure that we're not saying no to the Lord. Maybe we've had some prejudices, and maybe we have some things in our heart that aren't right. And God has been talking to us, asking us to put them aside and to put him first.

Peter didn't have to have God pound him over the head or to work with him for a year or six months or whatever. He had one vision, and he got the message, and he acted immediately. He changed his whole lifestyle, his whole way of thinking. He'd always been taught these things, and now Peter makes an about-face.

We have to obey God.

I think when we say, "Not so, Lord," it's often because of incomplete surrender. It's much like the old homesteaders who just didn't want to give up. The old homesteaders went out and they got on land. My parents did that out in western South Dakota. They homesteaded, and they had a right to that land because they staked their claim, and they lived on that claim, and that was their land. They were homesteaders.

But there's also what we call squatters who get on other people's property and try to take it. And that's what we are when we don't surrender to Jesus Christ—we're squatters. Because my body belongs to Jesus Christ, and when I tell God that I'm going to do what I want and be my own quarterback and live my own life, I'm a squatter and I'm taking God's property. That's what he tells us in 1 Corinthians 6: "Haven't you yet learned your body is the home of the Holy Spirit God gave you, and that he lives within you?" Your own body does not belong to you.

I'll say also that when we say that a woman has a right to abort because it's her body, and she can do as she wants, we're going contrary to this word from God, because a woman's body doesn't belong to that woman, and a man's body doesn't belong to that man, but to God. That's what he's telling us: "Your body does not belong to you, for God has bought you with a great price. So every part of your body is to give glory back to God, because he owns it" (1 Corinthians 6:19-20 in *The Living Bible*).

So sometimes we say no to the Lord because we have inadequate knowledge. As Americans, we don't realize that we don't own ourselves; we don't have perfect liberty, because this body is purchased by the blood of Jesus Christ, and we don't have a right to do what we want with it.

I remember talking to a young boy in the Brown County jail. He's in there for possession of drugs. I tried to point out how it was so wrong and how he was destroying himself. And he said, "I can do with my body what I want. And if I want to use drugs, I have every right to use it."

I said, "What about your parents? What about your sisters? What about the whole society you're going to affect? What about God, who owns your body?"

We don't have a right to destroy our body, and we don't have a right to misuse it and not use it in the King's service.

So sometimes we don't understand these things, and I think we say no to God because of it.

The last reason I think we say no to God is that we don't trust him. To one degree or another, there's not enough trust. So God asks us to do something, and we say, "No, sir, I'm not going to do it. I don't think that you can carry that out, I don't think that you can see us through, and I'm going to say no to God because I don't trust him enough." But God has all the answers, he has all the power, and that's what we have to see.

I read the story of a pastor named John McNeil. He was one of the great preachers of Scotland. He used to tell the story of how he was going one day to see a little old lady. She lived in a very poor flat in a very dingy part of town in Glasgow. He was going to visit her, and when he rang the doorbell, there was no answer. He knocked on the door again and again—no answer. He thought, "I know that this dear soul is here. She can't go anywhere, she's not able to travel." So he peeped through the keyhole, and there was this little soul sitting as quiet as a mouse.

So he just cracked the door a little bit, and he called inside, "I want to come in. It's your pastor, I want to see you."

She welcomed him in, and she said, "Oh, Pastor McNeil, it's you. I was afraid it was the landlord to collect the rent, and I didn't have any."

She didn't know that this was exactly why Pastor McNeil had come. He had the rent money for her in his pocket. Yet she—in her lack of knowledge—was afraid to let him in.

I think that happens so often. We say no to God, we say no to his Word, we say no to his Spirit, because we just can't see our way through, and we're not too sure that he's able to carry us and to take us through.

But God will never call us to do anything he can't supply and help us with. And he'll never call us into a place that's too big for us. But maybe there's a subconscious mind behind us saying, "Dear God, I just can't trust you that much. I'm just not that sure." So we have to lean on Jesus, we have to trust in Jesus. Put your whole weight on him.

I remember reading the story of a man who said that this really came to him one time because he was caught out on a little island with just a tiny boat like a canoe, and the tide was coming in. He knew that the tide would go well over his head, and he didn't have any paddles or sails or anything, and the canoe seemed so small. But there was only one thing he could do—just lie down in that canoe and let the tide come in. It came, and it raised him up and kept him safe.

That's what God does. He's that great ark of salvation, like the boat that Noah built and that saved his family. God is that ark, and from within that ark God says, "Come inside." And you know something, dear friend? We're told in the Scriptures that after God told him to enter that ark, and he gave them a certain period of time for going in, God shut the ark's door. Noah didn't shut the door, God shut the door.

God tells us to get into Jesus Christ, and he tells us to lean on Jesus and rest in Jesus. And if we will, he's able to save us unto the uttermost of time and the uttermost of sin, and he will keep us, and he will help us. But you have to do that, dear friend—you have to come to him. Because one of these days, God is going to close the door.

I've seen that in my ministry over and over—where people have had many opportunities to come to the Lord but they always refused, as far as I know. And I hope that in the last minute they called on the name of the Lord. But so far as I have any knowledge, they never turned to God, and there came a day when he closed the door, and that was the end.

So don't say no to God—say yes to God. Wherever he's leading us, whatever he's calling us to do, trust him, trust him fully.

Dear heavenly Father, we know that you're trustworthy. You've proved that to us over and over, a thousand times over. And we just love you, dear Lord, and we call you our Lord, and we make you our Lord. Help us just to love you and serve you all the days of our life. We pray these things in Jesus's name, amen.

GO AND TELL

John 20:19-23

The same day at evening, being the first day of the week, when the doors were shut where the disciples were assembled for fear of the Jews, Jesus came and stood in the midst and said to them, "Peace be with you." When He had said this, He showed them His hands and His side. Then the disciples were glad when they saw the Lord.

So Jesus said to them again, "Peace to you! As the Father has sent Me, I also send you." And when He had said this, He breathed on them, and said to them, "Receive the Holy Spirit. If you forgive the sins of any, they are forgiven them; if you retain the sins of any, they are retained."

THIS SCRIPTURE IS USUALLY READ ON EASTER SUNDAY. And you know that on that first Easter Sunday morning, two women came hurrying to the tomb—Mary Magdalene and "the other Mary," as Matthew calls her. And they came not to see a risen Christ but to see his final resting place, because they knew he had died on the cross, and they expected him to be in that tomb. But when they got there, the huge stone at the mouth of the sepulchre had been rolled back, and sitting upon that stone was a shining, brilliant, dazzling angel. And that angel spoke to the two women and said, "I know you came to see Jesus who was crucified. Well, he isn't here; he's risen just as he said." And then that angel gave them a message and he told those women, "Go and tell the disciples."

So there you have it, for all of us who name the name of Christ—we are to "go and tell."

The women were obedient to the angel's command, and they took off to tell the disciples. But to their astonishment, they met the risen Christ themselves. And what they didn't know is that Jesus Christ was going to give them the same command that the angel just shortly before had given them. Jesus commanded them, "Go and tell my brethren." And to the credit of these dear women, they obeyed. They went and they told.

Go and tell—let's look at that for a few minutes.

Go where? Well, for one thing we ought to go to our friends. We ought to go to all those we know and tell them about Jesus Christ, the risen Christ, and what he means to us, and what he's done for us. That's what Andrew did. He found Christ, and then the first thing he did afterward was to go to his brother Simon Peter, and Andrew brought him to Jesus.

And I ought to do the same great thing as they did with the gospel. I need to share it with my brothers, my sisters, my family, my friends, and all the other people I come in contact with. I need to share the gospel.

The apostle Paul tells us what that gospel is. He says in 1 Corinthians 15, "I delivered unto you first of all that which I also received, that Christ died for our sins, that he was buried, and that he arose again the third day." That's the gospel in a nutshell: Christ died, he was buried, and he was raised—he's the risen Christ.

We tell it to our friends, and we tell it to our kindred, we tell it to our acquaintances, we tell it to our schoolmates, our neighbors, our fellow employees, and our employers. We always need to be talking about Jesus.

Jesus then said in Matthew 28, "Go ye therefore and teach all nations, baptizing them in the name of the Father, and of the Son, and of the Holy Spirit, teaching them to observe all things whatsoever I have commanded you. And lo, I am with you always, even unto the end of the world or the end of the age."

So the command from the Son of God is clear as a bell: "I want you to go and I want you to tell." Tell the world the good news of the gospel. It rests in our hands, it rests in the hands of the redeemed. It's our mission. It's not the mission of the world to go and tell—it's the mission of the redeemed, of the disciples of Jesus Christ. That's our work. Jesus tells us to go and tell the good news, because it's the only hope of the soul.

We see this very plainly in John 20:19-23, where we read, "Then the same day at evening, being the first day of the week, when the doors were shut where the disciples were assembled for fear of the Jews, Jesus came and stood in their midst and said unto them, 'Peace be unto you.'"

Then he showed them his hands and his side, and then the disciples were glad when they saw the Lord. Then Jesus said to them again, "Peace be unto you. As my Father had sent me, even so send I you." And then he breathed on them and said, "Receive the Holy Spirit." And then Jesus said, "Whose ever sins you remit, they are remitted unto them. And whose ever sins you retain, they are retained."

Let's look closer at this passage in John 20. Jesus appears to the disciples not in a public place but in a locked and closed private room. And many believe it was the same upper room where he'd eaten with his disciples on the night before he died. John says that the doors were locked and bolted, and yet Jesus appears in the midst of them without touching a lock or key or anything else. He was there among them.

These disciples were just amazed, and they're wondering, "Is this a ghost? Is this a spirit? Is this an apparition? What is this in our midst?" There were only ten of the twelve disciples there. Judas was gone, and Thomas was absent, so just ten were there. They were gathered together with the doors bolted and locked, and their hearts filled with fear, because there was an awful hatred among the Jewish leaders in that day and that hour. They had just put Jesus Christ on the cross, and who knows, they might wish to do the same to his disciples. In that awful, terrible hostility toward the teachings of Christ, they might put to death all of his followers. The followers didn't know, so they had fear with good cause.

Now they're together, but at the crucifixion these men had run for their lives. They'd scattered like sheep without a shepherd. But after a while, as they're hearing about the possibility of a resurrection, they come together, and they can't believe it. And maybe they don't believe it, but they've got to see each other, and they've got to talk together.

That's what Christian people do, don't they? We seek each other out. We're not looking for the world, we're looking for other believers. That's why we gather together, because we need each other, and we love each other.

So they gathered together to talk about these events. The women had told them about what happened, and Peter and John told of their experience, and the whole group of them were just wondering about this resurrection. They were like the two disciples on the road to Emmaus—you remember that they were walking along, and Jesus joined them. They were talking, and they didn't know who Jesus was as he talked with them. And Jesus asks them what they're talking about, and they say, "Don't you know the things that are happening?" And Jesus replies, "What things?" Then they answered, "Concerning Jesus of Nazareth, a prophet mighty in deed and word. We hoped that it was he who would redeem Israel." And so in their despondency and despair they are talking about this on the road to Emmaus.

They probably did the same there in the upper room that night. There's a kind of a despair about it all, and yet they're talking about a resurrection. That's what they were doing that night. That first Easter Sunday evening, they gathered together as a pitiful little group of people, scared half to death to talk about Jesus who was crucified and dead.

Then they're startled, because suddenly Jesus Christ is in the very midst of them. It's unbelievable, and they wonder if they're dreaming. Is this a ghost or something? Is this a trick? But it's true, they see that it's true—this is Jesus, beyond any doubt. He had come to them in a supernatural way without opening the door or turning a lock, he's there in their midst. There he was in person, and he speaks to them. And the first thing he says is, "Shalom. Peace be unto you."

Oh, my soul, I'm going to tell you that peace is the one thing they didn't have. They didn't have peace in their soul. There was turmoil, and they still thought about Gethsemane, they still thought about the cross. They still thought about the darkness at noonday, and they thought about the earthquake. They thought about the tearing of that huge veil that may have weighed three hundred pounds, that huge veil torn in two in the Holy of Holies in the temple. They thought about the earthquake, and the tombs opening, and the people coming out, the saints coming out of the tombs and walking around old Jerusalem.

So they didn't have peace at heart. They were filled with questions and despair and fear.

So Jesus said, "Peace be unto you." That's what Jesus always tells us. He says, "I don't want you to be afraid. I want you to lean on me. I want you to put all the weight of your burdens on me. I don't want you to be always figuring and manipulating and trying to work out how this or that is going to be. Don't be afraid—peace be unto you."

And after Jesus said that, we're told that the disciples were so glad when they saw the Lord, and their fear was gone. Then Jesus says again, "Peace be unto you," only this time he adds something to it. He says,

"Peace, peace be unto you," and then he says, "As my Father has sent me, even so send I you."

Now, he's talking there to all of us. He's not talking just to a few people in that upper room. He's talking to you and to me. If you name the name of Christ, he's talking to you: "So send I you. As my Father sent me, now I am sending you." And he's reminding them about the cross. Because he then showed them his hands and he showed them his side—he showed them those scars. And what Jesus is saying is, "Now I'm going to send you. As the Father sent me, I'm going to send you—but it's going to cost you something."

He showed them the scars. And he's telling them that the way of the scars is the way of the cross, and it's the way of suffering, and it's the way of self-denial. It's the way of hardship and hardness and the giving of self in sacrifice. Jesus Christ is showing us the scars, and he's saying, "Are you willing to follow me as I followed my Father? Will you suffer for me, and will you deny yourself for me?" That's exactly what he's showing. He showed them his hands and his feet.

Then he breathed on them, and he said unto them, "Receive ye the Holy Spirit." Now that was a symbolic gesture. He didn't give them the Holy Spirit at that time, we know that. That was yet something to come. Forty days later, Jesus ascended into heaven, and then forty days later he sent the Holy Spirit and they received the Holy Spirit and we call it Pentecost.

So he didn't give them the Holy Spirit at this time, he just in symbolic form said, "You're going to get the Holy Spirit. I want you to serve me in all the world, and I'm going to give you the strength to do it; I'm going to give you my Spirit. And I won't ask you to do anything that I don't give you the strength to do."

Jesus asks us to do a lot of things, and sometimes we stagger at the thought of them. But we ought to remember that he never gives us anything that he won't prepare us for first. He never gives us anything to do that he won't equip us for, and help us as we do it. Maybe we've never done it before.

I think of these parents with their little babies. One new mother got her little baby in the hospital. At home, she had a new washer and a new dryer, and she had a little book of instructions on how to run all these appliances. So she asked the doctor if there was a little book that came with the baby. "You see, I've never been a mother before, and my husband has never been a father before. What am I going to do?" Well, if God gives you a child, he'll help you to take care of that child, if you're open to the Lord and love the Lord.

Jesus tells them the reason he is sending them. They have to go because there's a lost world. He tells them that he will give them the power of God to go, and he tells them the purpose for their being sent. And he says, "Whose ever sins you forgive, they are forgiven unto them. And whose ever sins you retain, they are retained."

Now this Scripture has surely been misunderstood and misappropriated, and sometimes you hear clergy running around as if they're going to forgive sin. But anybody knows, if they read anything of the New Testament at all, that the only one who can forgive sins is Jesus Christ, period. And if you don't remember anything else from this chapter, remember this: Jesus Christ is the only answer to the sins of the world.

This means that Jesus came to forgive sins. That's what they said when he was born. They were told to call his name Jesus, "because he will save his people from their sins." That's the reason he came, and God gave him the authority to forgive sins.

Then Jesus said, "As the Father has given me this authority and has sent me out, so send I you." Jesus is saying that he has all authority and all the power. "I'm going to send you, and you're to go out into all the world, and you tell them about Jesus Christ. You tell them about me."

What he's saying is this: "I'm giving you the gospel—that's the keys to the kingdom. I'm giving you this gospel of Christ. And you're to go into the world, and you preach the gospel, and you teach it in Sunday school classes and wherever, and you teach it to your children at home. I'm going to give you this key."

Now, when you go and preach about Jesus and his power to save, and people put their faith in Jesus, you can say, "Your sins are forgiven." I've said it hundreds of times to people in their home or in the hospital, after they pray to receive Jesus. I say, "Your sins are forgiven." I'm not forgiving their sins, I'm just telling them, "I am preaching the gospel, and if you accept Jesus Christ, your sins are forgiven." If I talk to somebody about their soul, which I have done, and they refuse to accept Jesus, then I can say, "Your sins are retained. You still have those sins, and you will die in them. And if you die in them, you'll go to a Christless eternity."

So we have to share the gospel, every one of us. And if anyone receives the gospel, they're safe. If they reject that gospel, they're not safe. It's for us to tell the good news to the lost in love and forgiveness and kindness—that's our mission.

I was reading the other day about John Ehrlichman and Charles Colson, and you remember their story of Watergate. They were embroiled in this awful Watergate scandal that led to the humiliating resignation of President Nixon. And both men, Ehrlichman and Colson, spent time in prison because of their part in Watergate. While in prison, Colson accepted Christ and became a Christian. Ehrlichman, a Christian Scientist, never turned to God. He only became bitter, and he seethed in his anger, as the story goes.

For over twenty years Ehrlichman despised Colson, and he couldn't say enough mean things about him. He wrote defamatory articles against Colson, and he was just so bitter and so hard toward this man.

Less than a year before John Ehrlichman died in 1999, Charles Colson learned of Ehrlichman's failing health and went to see him. There he was, dying of renal failure—this man who was once domestic affairs supervisor and adviser to the president, and whose office was just directly above the Oval Office. He'd held such a high position, but now here he was in a nursing home, after his third wife had left him, and he was alienated from his children. And Charles Colson comes to this bitter old man on the verge of death, and he tells him about Jesus Christ. Ehrlichman didn't accept Christ, but later he said he was amazed by Colson's love and forgiveness and sharing about Jesus Christ. He just couldn't get over it.

Finally Ehrlichman called Colson and said, "The doctors tell me it's just a matter of days. I'm not going to live much longer." Colson was ill himself and he couldn't go to Ehrlichman, but he called a trusted friend and asked that friend to go and talk to John Ehrlichman. His friend went, and Ehrlichman received Jesus Christ. And shortly thereafter, he entered into the presence of God—because one Christian extended love and forgiveness to him. Genuine forgiveness and genuine love are powerful.

But this is the point: Charles Colson was holding the key, and he used that key on behalf of John Ehrlichman's soul. And Ehrlichman's sins were taken away—not by Colson, but by Christ. Colson had the key—Christ *was* the key, and the gospel is the key. And Ehrlichman is in heaven today because Colson shared with this man who'd been so bitter toward him.

Colson might have kept that key to himself and refused to share it, especially to an enemy, a man that had been so bitter and critical toward him. If he had kept that key to himself and refused to share it, Ehrlichman would be in hell today.

In that sense, and in that sense alone, we have the keys to the kingdom. That's why we must go out into all the world, because we have the answer, we have the keys. We have the power in our hands to show others the way of eternal life. We don't give them that life, but we bring them to the person who gives them that life, and that's our responsibility.

We have the power to help deliver people from a Christless eternity, but if we don't share it—if we curl up in the corner and keep it to ourselves and we never reach out to a lost world—we are going to be guilty, and we're going to have their sin retained, because you and I didn't go. We'll be guilty of their soul being cast into hell, because we had the message and we had the keys, but failed to share it.

That's why it has to be done. It's got to be done. So may God help every one of us to heed this gospel of God that he has given us. May you respond liberally and cheerfully to the word of the Lord: "As the Father has sent me, even so send I you."

Jesus is telling every one of us today: "You go, and you tell." That's our business, that's our mission.

Heavenly Father, thank you that we have a wonderful gospel. We thank you that there were those who shared the gospel with us. I'm thankful that so long ago, Vernon Eggebraaten shared the gospel with me, and I accepted you, and my sins were all taken away—not by that evangelist, but because he told me about Jesus. So help us to share the gospel, to be looking for every way that we can share it, because we have the answer. And if we want to give it to them, they can have it and be saved. If we keep it to ourselves, they'll be lost. Help us to be obedient to your command, to go and tell. In Jesus's name, amen.

A Further Word

JESUS IS COMING AGAIN

1 Thessalonians 4:13-18

But I do not want you to be ignorant, brethren, concerning those who have fallen asleep, lest you sorrow as others who have no hope. For if we believe that Jesus died and rose again, even so God will bring with Him those who sleep in Jesus. For this we say to you by the word of the Lord, that we who are alive and remain until the coming of the Lord will by no means precede those who are asleep. For the Lord Himself will descend from heaven with a shout, with the voice of an archangel, and with the trumpet of God. And the dead in Christ will rise first. Then we who are alive and remain shall be caught up together with them in the clouds to meet the Lord in the air. And thus we shall always be with the Lord. Therefore comfort one another with these words.

I LOVE TO PREACH ABOUT THE LOVE OF GOD, BECAUSE God loves you. But watch out. There's an end to the love of God. If you refuse his Son Jesus, the wrath of God is going to be poured on you. That's what we're told in the Scriptures. If we receive him, we have everlasting life; if we reject him, we have everlasting condemnation.

I just pray that you know that God loves you so much that he gave his Son to die for you, and he's not willing that any should perish, but that all should come to repentance. But if you don't come, then he can't take you into heaven, because heaven is a perfect place, and nobody's perfect.

We all have some imperfection, some sin. And so we come to Jesus, and he covers us with his righteousness, and we're made perfect, because we're in Christ. You have to ask Jesus into your heart, and to save you from your sins. I hope you'll do that, because God's love will never end for those who belong to him.

Shortly before Jesus ascended into heaven, he told his disciples what would take place. He said that he'd leave them, and he'd go to the Father, and that when he got there, he would prepare a place for them. He said that he'd send the Holy Spirit. The Holy Spirit would be a comforter, and stand by them, and strengthen them and help them. And so, he would be with them until they got to heaven.

And then one of the apostles, Thomas—people call him Doubting Thomas, but I call him honest Thomas—he had a question, he had a doubt, and he admitted it, so I call him honest Thomas.

When Thomas talks to Jesus about heaven, he says, "Yes, heaven. It must be a wonderful place. And yes, I want to go to heaven. If you're there, Jesus, I want to be with you in heaven, and I want to be with the rest of your disciples, and I want to be with the people of God. Yes, I want to go to heaven." Then Thomas says, "But I don't know how to get there. I don't have a road map. I don't have any way to get there. What am I going to do?"

Listen to our dear Savior, as he speaks to Thomas—and to the whole wide world. Jesus said unto him, "I am the way to heaven. I am the way, the truth, and the life. No man cometh unto the Father, but by me." That's John 14, verse 6.

Praise God, then—there's a way to heaven, there's a road to heaven, and the way is as plain as the nose on your face. The way is Jesus.

I love the church, and I spend my life in the church. But the church can't save you or me or anyone, because the church isn't the way to heaven. Jesus is the way to heaven. You need to have a church, and you ought to be in a church or at least support a church where the Bible is taught and preached. But the church can't get you into heaven.

Jesus said, "I'm the way." The apostle Peter puts it this way, in Acts 4, verse 12: "Neither is there salvation in any other: there is none other name under heaven given among men, whereby we must be saved."

Now, it's a fact that the world is full of people telling you how to get to heaven. All the religions are always telling you how to get to heaven. They're all over the place. They're just like fleas on a dog's back.

But the Bible tells us in Proverbs 14, verse 12: "There is a way which seemeth right unto a man, but the end thereof are the ways of death." Jesus tells us so that no one needs to miss it. Listen to this—in John 3:36, this is Jesus talking, this Jesus who loves you and died for you: "He that believeth on the Son hath everlasting life, and he that believeth not the Son shall not see life." Listen to Jesus.

You've got to have Jesus. "I am the way," Jesus said. He starts this fourteenth chapter of John's Gospel by saying, "Believe in God, believe also in me." He's saying it in so many words: "If you believe in God, that's not enough. You believe in God, you've got to believe in me. You have to believe in me, because I am the way, and there's no other way to God."

If you want to get to God, then the road to God is through Jesus Christ, who tells us, "I am the door. I'm the way."

So we urge people to put their faith in Jesus, to put their trust in him. I'm praying to God that you won't miss it. Maybe right now you'll pray, "Dear Jesus, I'm a sinner. I just ask you to come into my heart, and to take away my sin. I want to go to heaven. I want to be with you. I don't want to face the wrath of God, because I know the Bible says that it's a fearful thing to fall into the hands of an angry God." I tremble for you, friend. Come to Jesus. You can do it right this minute.

Then Jesus tells his disciples, "I will come again." There's going to be a time when Jesus will return to earth again—someday. He says that in 1 Thessalonians 4. He says, "I'm going to come again. I will come again." That's what we call the rapture, and he describes it perfectly in this passage. What this rapture simply means is the time when Jesus comes for his people. I'll talk about that a little bit more later in this chapter.

But I want you first of all to see that Paul is writing to the churches at Thessalonica, and many of them had accepted the Lord, and then some of them had died. And the others had questions as they all looked for Jesus to come again. They were saying, "Well, if we die, how can we be with Jesus? And when Jesus comes again, and he takes us to be with himself, if we've already died, what's going to happen to us? Will we have any part in the kingdom of God? What are we going to do?"

That was a big problem with them. So, the apostle Paul talks about them in this passage, and he tells them what will happen when the Lord Jesus comes again. Yes, that moment that they die, they're going to go to the grave, but Jesus is going to come again, and he's going to raise them from the dead, and they're going to rule and reign with Christ, along with all who believe.

Paul writes about it, and he starts out by saying, "I would not have you to be ignorant"—that is, uninformed. He's saying, "I don't want you to be uninformed about this matter." And this matter, he says, is "concerning them which are asleep, that you sorrow not even as those who have no hope."

Paul is telling the Thessalonians, "I don't want you to be ignorant or uninformed about this matter, and I'm going to spell it out for you." So he tells them exactly what's going to happen. He gets all his information from God, because he says, "This is the word of the Lord." The Lord himself has given these words. And what the Bible says is the only reliable information we can have about what happens after we die.

If you put your faith in Jesus, listen to what God has to say! So Paul is saying, "I'm going to write this, so that you don't sorrow like others who have no hope." He says, "I don't want you to be like the heathen, because when one of them dies, they don't know what will happen, or whether they'll never see each other again. They have no hope. But we have a hope, and we profit from this hope, because it gives us courage, and it gives us strength."

Then he says, "This answer I want you to know, this is what God says." In verse 15 of this passage, we read, "We say unto you by the word of the Lord"—and so just take it for that. You can count on it, because it's what God is saying, and that's what God is doing. So watch out for your source of information. Now, I don't know what you believe. I don't know what your faith is. There are some people who'll say, "Well, if you're just sincere, you'll go to heaven."

Well, I read about a man who got up in the night, and he had a severe headache. He didn't want to wake up his wife, and so he thought he'd get some aspirin tablets. When he took the aspirin tablets, they weren't aspirin tablets, they were strychnine. He took them believing they were aspirin tablets, and he had all this faith in them that they were aspirin tablets, but he died.

You see, you can believe something as strongly as ever, but still be totally wrong. You can have your faith in something that still leads to death and to hell. So put your faith in the Lord Jesus Christ.

And then Paul says, "The Lord himself shall descend from heaven with a shout and with the voice of the archangel, and with the trump of God, and the dead in Christ shall rise first." He's talking about those who are asleep in Jesus, and when you have that word *sleep*, it just simply means that the body is resting in the grave. The spirit and soul are going to be with the Lord. The spirit and soul of your loved one are not in the grave.

When a Christian dies, we're told that the spirit is absent from the body, but at home with the Lord. And the minute we die, we're going to be with the Lord and to rest in him. It's called sleep because of the stillness of the body. It's called sleep because the body is resting from its labors and the struggles of life. It's called sleep because it's only temporary, because it's going to be awakened again.

The word used in Greek is *koimeterion*, and it means a sleeping place; that's what a cemetery is, a sleeping place. As John Stott says, "Cemeteries are dormitories of the dead."[26] The thing to keep in mind is that when Paul talks about sleep, he's not talking about soul sleep, but about the body being placed out in the cemetery, and how it rests there until the Lord comes again.

So we don't worry when we're in Christ, as those who have no hope. We have that wonderful hope in Jesus, and we rejoice in him, and we lean upon him. We rejoice because we know where that person is.

I read about a man whose wife died and people said to him, "I feel sorry that you lost your wife." And the man said, "I didn't lose my wife. I know where she is. She's in heaven." They had that hope, that glorious hope.

And so, Paul talks about it, and here's what he says in verse 16: "The Lord himself shall descend from heaven with a shout, with the voice of the archangel, and with the trump of God." The Lord himself will come—he's not going to send an angel, he's not going to send somebody else, but he's coming himself, in person, in the flesh. Now, there are some people who'll say, "Well, Jesus meant that he'll come when we die, that he is coming again and coming by a spirit."

But listen to what the angel tells the men of Galilee, when Jesus has just ascended into heaven. The angel comes to them and says, " Ye men of Galilee, why stand ye gazing up into heaven? This same Jesus, which is taken up from you into heaven, shall so come in like manner as ye have seen him go into heaven."

It's as clear as a bell. This same Jesus, who ascended into heaven, is going to come back again. He shall descend from heaven. He's now sitting at the right hand of God in heaven, but he's going to come back to this earth, and he's going to come for all believers, for his children, his body, his church—for those who receive him, those who are born again.

When people talk about being born again, don't let that frighten you off. It's just a new birth, it's a second birth, it's regeneration, it's a birth from above. It all means the same thing. It is what happens when we ask Jesus into our life to take away our sin. That's what it means. And all of those who believe in Jesus are going to be caught up. Now, this is at a later date, at another time. Jesus is going to come to this earth with his saints, with his people. In this 1 Thessalonians 4 passage, he's coming for his people to take them out of the earth, to meet them in the air.

Then later on, he will come with his saints, and his feet will touch the earth. We read about that in Zechariah 14, where we're told of the day when Jesus returns to earth: "On that day, His feet shall stand in Mount of Olives, east of Jerusalem, and the Mount of Olives will be split into two from east to west, forming a great valley and half of the mountain moving north, half moving the south." Now, this is not happening in the text that we're reading in 1 Thessalonians 4, where we're caught up to meet the Lord in the air. In Zechariah, it's when he comes again, and his feet touch the earth, and he sets up his glorious kingdom.

He comes with a shout that's the shout of command. He commands the dead in Christ to come forth. You see that in Lazarus. Remember

Lazarus in the grave? Jesus comes when Lazarus had been in the grave four days, and Jesus is going to raise Lazarus, and he calls and he says, "Lazarus, come forth." And Lazarus has to come forth. Now look at Lazarus. He had lived once, he'd died once, he'd gone to heaven once, he was in heaven rejoicing with God and the holy angels and all of the glories of heaven. He was so happy—and he had to give it up and come back to earth.

Jesus makes the command. He says, "Lazarus, come forth." So Lazarus comes forth, he's raised from the dead. He will live again, he will have to die again, and then go to heaven again. And Lazarus says, "Well, here I go again."

But the point is the great power of God Almighty—and Jesus calls Lazarus out. That's what we need to know, because we're told in the Scriptures, in John 5:28-29, "The hour is coming, in which all that are in the graves shall hear his voice, and shall come forth." All of the Christians will come forth. All those dear believers who have died in Uganda, and all those in Iraq, and all over the world. They're dead in Christ, but they'll be raised up, and we'll see them from all over the world and from out of the sea, and out of the flood, and out of the fire, and out of the Colosseum in Rome. They'll be raised up through the great power of God Almighty, with the voice of the archangel. I wonder if it's Michael? We don't know who it is, and it doesn't matter. There's going to be the resurrection.

Then Paul talks about the Christian dead. He says, "The dead in Christ arise first," that's in verse 16. And the spirit and the soul come from heaven, because when we die, we're absent from the body, but at home with the Lord. The moment we die, we're in the presence of God, that same instant. So, we're with the Lord, and now he's going to bring us back, and we're going to have that spirit and soul.

The spirit and soul are immortal. No matter what you do, the soul is immortal, and it's going to live forever either in heaven or hell. It's immortal. The body is mortal, but that mortal body is going to become immortal, and that which is corruptible is going to become incorruptible. That mortal body is going to become an immortal body, with spirit and soul, and with the Lord forever.

Like Nicodemus, we might say, "Well, how can these things be? How can these things happen?" Think about it this way. Paul talks about when a kernel of corn is planted, and the corn dies, but from that dead kernel comes a new kernel. So the body is like seeds sown in a planted ground. The seed dies, but from that death comes a new body.

After Jesus was risen, his disciples recognized his resurrected body, and they'll recognize yours, and they'll recognize mine. Only it will be an improved body. He'll make some improvements. We won't have pains and defects like that. He'll fix us up, and won't that be something! But we have to wait for the resurrection. So the kernel of corn is not the identical seed that was planted; the new seed is the same as that sown, though it's different, because the original died, and the new is there. And in the wonderful resurrection of Christ, he gives us the power and the ability to do that.

Then Paul talks about what happens with the living. The dead will be raised, and now he speaks of the Christians that are living, in verse 17. He says, "Then we which are alive and remain shall be caught up together with them in the clouds, to meet the Lord in the air: so shall we ever be with the Lord."

When you read the Bible, there's the Greek word *rapto*, which we call the rapture. That's what Paul is talking about here, when the living Christians are caught up to meet the Lord in the air. That's the teaching, so call it what you want. Now, the Greek word means to seize or to carry off. So, the Lord seizes us, he takes us, he carries us to be with him into glory.

In the Bible, this word *rapto* is used several ways. It means to carry away speedily in the passage where Philip was in Samaria preaching. God wanted him in another place, and all of a sudden, he's preaching to the Ethiopian eunuch in a totally different place. It also means to seize by force, where he just takes us without a thought. It's used when Lot was in Sodom. Sodom and Gomorrah were such desperately wicked and horrible places that God wiped them off the face of the earth. But Lot was saved, and God seized him, he just took by force, and brought Lot out of Sodom and saved him, because Lot was a believer and he trusted God. And so we will be taken up to meet the Lord in the air and be with the Lord.

Let me close by talking about three wonderful truths we learn from this passage. First of all, we can comfort and encourage one another. That's what Paul says: "Wherefore, comfort one another with these words."

So many times I've seen people who are really suffering, they're discouraged, they're downhearted. I've been in a nursing home or retirement home, and I've seen some of these dear, dear wonderful people, and the hard times they have. If you see such as these, give them a word of encouragement, give them a pat on the back. Give them a hug. Tell them you're praying for them. Tell them, "God bless you."

Look around and see how many people you can help. Comfort one another, God says. That's your business. Don't be such an old sourpuss, like you've been baptized in pickle juice. Cheer up; things aren't that bad, after all. Comfort one another.

The second thing is that we're going to see our loved ones again. I get letters all the time, and they will ask, "Will we know our loved ones in heaven?" Of course we will. Absolutely." We'll know Jesus, and we'll know all of our loved ones.

And third, we'll be with the Lord forever. Jesus promised: "Where I am, there you may be also." So, we'll see Jesus face to face, this wonderful Lord who has loved and served and helped us in so many ways and stood by us. We're going to see him. We can see him in the Word of God, and we can see him in the hearts and lives of Christian people, but we really don't yet see his face. Paul talked about that in 1 Corinthians. He says, "For now we see through a glass, darkly; but then face to face. Now I know in part; but then shall I know even as also I am known." The *Good News Translation* has paraphrased it like this: "What we see now is like the dim image in a mirror; but then we shall see face to face. What I know now is partial; then we will know complete—as complete as God's knowledge of me."

And that's what we're going to do. We're going to see Christ. Won't that be a wonderful day! Just think about the time when you'll meet the Lord!

There's a hymn with a chorus that goes like this:

It will be worth it all when we see Jesus.
Life's trials will seem so small when we see Christ.
One glimpse of his dear face

all sorrow will erase.

So bravely run the race till we see Christ.[27]

I want to close this book by asking this, dear friend: Do you know Jesus? Have you accepted Jesus? You've got to have him. I beg of you to come to Jesus. Don't put it off.

You may say, "Well, I don't know if I'm ready for him. I don't know if I'm ready to meet him or not. I don't know."

Well, if you're not sure, let me ask you to write this verse down: John 5:24. This verse has these words of Jesus: "Verily, verily, I say unto you, he that heareth my word, and believeth on him that sent me, hath everlasting life."

You have everlasting life at the minute you ask him into your heart!

And there's more: "He that heareth my word, and believeth on him that sent me, hath everlasting life and shall not come into condemnation, but is passed from death unto life."

You won't go to hell—that is what Jesus is saying. You have to have Jesus. So I pray that you put your faith in the Lord Jesus. Just say this prayer:

"Dear Lord Jesus, I'm a sinner, and I ask you to come into my heart and take away my sin. And Lord Jesus, I'll forsake that sin the best I can, and I'll serve you the best I can. I'll make you the Lord in my life. I just love you, and I ask you to save me from my sin." And then you thank him: "Thank you, dear Jesus, for coming into my life, thank you for making me a child of God. Thank you for writing my name in the Lamb's book of life. Thank you, thank you."

And if you do that, I'll see you in heaven, and together we will look into the beautiful, beautiful face of Jesus. To know him is to love him.

Dear heavenly Father, thank you for the Savior. Thank you that he loves us all. He's not willing that any should perish. Thank you for the wonderful future we have. The trumpet will sound, and the dead in Christ will be raised, and we'll be caught up to meet the Lord in the air. That's going to happen just as sure as the sun comes up in the east. It's going to happen. Help us to be ready. Help us to love you and trust you, and all glory goes to the Son. In Jesus's name, amen.

ENDNOTES

1   G. Campbell Morgan, "The Exalted Christ," in "Sermons on the Resurrection" available at The Gospel Truth website, at this link: https://bit.ly/37so2NS.

2   Exact source unknown.

3   See the "Todd Beamer" article by Douglas Holt in the September 20, 2001 edition of the *Los Angeles Times*. Available at http://lat.ms/3bne8Op.

4   Evan Thomas, "Their Faith and Fears," *Newsweek*, September 8, 2002. Available at http://bit.ly/3ue0h5D.

5   Lisa Beamer with Ken Abraham, *Let's Roll! Ordinary People, Extraordinary Courage* (Tyndale, 2002).

6   Marcus Dods, *The Expositor's Bible: The Gospel of St. John*, vol. I, p. 175. Available here: http://bit.ly/3uuUr05.

7   As reported by the Associated Press. See the article published September 16, 2001, in the *Baltimore Sun*: "$231 Million in Gold, Silver Lies Beneath Tower Rubble." Available here: http://bit.ly/3swBjNe. See also "Crushed Towers Give Up Cache of Gold Ingots" by Nicholas Wapshott, a *Times Online* article (London's *The Times*) published November 1, 2001. Available here: http://911research.wtc7.net/cache/wtc/evidence/timesonline_gold.html.

8   Adrian Rogers, "Jesus Is God's Answer to Man's Disability," recorded sermon. Available here: https://bit.ly/2PfhN9Q.

9   *United States v. George Wilson*, January 26, 1833. Text of the decision available here: https://bit.ly/2PgVIYs. Wilson spent another decade in prison, but was never executed. He was finally pardoned again by President Martin Van Buren, and this time accepted it (see the news item of January 14, 1841, in the Philadelphia *National Gazette*, available here: https://www.newspapers.com/clip/68812431/george-wilson/. See also the March 13, 2019 article "History's Lone Refusal of Presidential Pardon" by journalist Charlie Smith, March 13, 2019, available here: https://www.columbianprogress.com/opinion-columns/historys-lone-refusal-presidential-pardon#sthash.SHIcwFoF.jeCnbeGx.dpbs.

10 Film clip from *You Don't Know Jack* (2010). Available at: https://www.youtube.com/watch?v=z1mquF-crAE.

11 D. L. Moody, "More Alive Than Ever," quotation available here: https://www.crossroad.to/Quotes/faith/moody.htm.

12   Comments from Dr. Benjamin Spock about spanking are available here: http://bit.ly/3l1qTTd.

13   J. C. Ryle. *Expository Thoughts on Matthew* (1856). Available here: http://bit.ly/3eyyJCE.

14   G. Campbell Morgan, *The Gospel According to Matthew* (1929). Available here: https://archive.org/details/in.ernet.dli.2015.89722.

15   G. Campbell Morgan, *The Gospel According to John* (1907). Available here: http://bit.ly/2PYemol.

16   Warren Wiersbe, "John 17," in the *Warren Weirsbe BE Bible Study Series.* Available here: http://bit.ly/30FePxD.

17   Anne Cetas, "A Bouquet of Praise," *Our Daily Bread,* February 17, 2011. Available here: https://bit.ly/3lieYAH.

18   Charles R. Swindoll, "Insights on John," in *Swindoll's Living Insights New Testament Commentary,* Book 4 (2014).

19   Merrill C. Tenney, *John: The Gospel of Belief* (1948), 248-249.

20   Warren Wiersbe, *Be Loyal (Matthew): Following the King of Kings* (1980), 270.

21   Warren Wiersbe, *Be Loyal,* 270.

22   Most often attributed to British congregational minister Joseph Parker, 1830-1902.

23   G. Campbell Morgan, *The Gospel According to Matthew.* Available here: https://bit.ly/2OLYnsP.

24   David C. Egner, "There When You Need It," *Our Daily Bread,* June 30, 1999. Available here: https://bit.ly/3cjq2t6.

25   Clarence E. MaCartney, "The Precious Blood of Christ," in his 1947 sermon series *The Greatest Texts of the Bible.*

26   John Stott, *The Message of 1 and 2 Thessalonians.* (InterVarsity Press, 1991), 96.

27   Esther Kerr Rusthoi, "It Will Be Worth It All," © 1941 by New Spring.